GW00359583

COLLINS
*Glasgow & London*

First published 1990

Copyright © William Collins Sons & Company Limited
Published by William Collins Sons & Company Limited

Printed in Hong Kong

ISBN 0 00 435783-3

# HOW TO USE THIS BOOK

Your Collins Traveller Guide will help you find your way around your chosen destination quickly and easily. It is colour-coded for easy reference:

The blue-coded 'topic' section answers the question 'I would like to see or do something; where do I go and what do I see when I get there?' A simple, clear layout provides an alphabetical list of activities and events, offers you a selection of each, tells you how to get there, what it will cost, when it is open and what to expect. Each topic in the list has its own simplified map, showing the position of each item and the nearest landmark or transport access, for instant orientation. Whether your interest is Architecture or Food you can find all the information you need quickly and simply. Where major resorts within an area require in-depth treatment, they follow the main topics section in alphabetical order.

The red-coded section is a lively and informative gazetteer. In one alphabetical list you can find essential facts about the main places and cultural items - 'What is La Bastille?', 'Who was Michelangelo?' - as well as practical and invaluable travel information. It covers everything you need to know to help you enjoy yourself and get the most out of your time away, from Accommodation through Babysitters, Car Hire, Food, Health, Money, Newspapers, Taxis and Telephones to Zoos.

Cross-references: Type in small capitals - **CHURCHES** - tells you that more information on an item is available within the topic on churches. A-Z in bold - **A-Z** - tells you that more information is available on an item within the gazetteer. Simply look under the appropriate heading. A name in bold - **Holy Cathedral** - also tells you that more information on an item is available in the gazetteer under that particular heading.

Packed full of information and easy to use - you'll always know where you are with your Collins Traveller Guide!

*Photographs by **Doug Corrance***

Paris brings the senses to life. As you walk through its streets and along its boulevards luscious displays of fish and oysters outside the brasseries tempt you. You will also be tempted by the pastries displayed in the patisseries and as you pass the pavement cafés the scent of coffee and *brioches*, and the cheerful clatter of that thick china on their zinc tabletops lures you in so that, sooner or later, you'll sit down at one of those tables. And, sitting at a table in one of the city's famous cafés with your coffee or *citron* you can indulge in the famous Parisian pastime of watching people going about their business.

And sooner or later, as you make your way about the city on the clean and efficient *Métro*, or as you stroll along the boulevards created by Napoléon's Baron Haussman, past shop windows in which elegance is sold as nowhere else, and among the people of whom that elegance is a hallmark, you can't help noticing the style and self-possession of the locals. Style is the birthright of the Parisian and Parisienne.

Paris is aptly named the 'City of Light', and to confirm that you will do well to go to the Musée d'Orsay where Impressionist and other French painters of the late 19thC and early 20thC are now displayed in what was once the Gare d'Orsay, the old railway station. Among the superb displays of sculptures and paintings (and for the Impressionists the interpretation of light was of paramount importance) you will see more style and begin to realise how Paris has passed on this inheritance to its present day citizens.

Paris is full of galleries and museums - the Louvre is within 500 metres of the Pont Royal across the Seine - but you will not want to go there so soon after the Musée d'Orsay. Instead stay on the Left Bank and walk upstream and turn right at the Place St Michel onto the Boulevard St Michel. Here you will find yourself in the heart of the Latin Quarter, the setting for Puccini's La Bohème. Here too you can see the history of Paris, medieval houses, the beautiful church of St Séverin begun in the 13thC, enlarged in the 16thC and then decorated in the 17th and 18th. And of course this area is home to the Sorbonne, one of the oldest, and still one of the leading, universities in the world.

Across the Boulevard St Germain is the Musée de Cluny, a 15thC house of great beauty which now holds a collection of incomparable tapestries, among them a group of six called Lady with the Unicorn,

which represent the five senses. By this time you will have gained a feel
for the city and in the days to come you are ready to relax and soak up
the atmosphere.

What could be more atmospheric than the open-air markets - the flea
market out at Clignancourt, held at the weekend, which sells everything from clothes to antiques; and in the true centre of Paris, where the
city began, you'll find the beautiful flower market on the Ile de la Cité.
But the Grands Magasins will give you a different impression of French
commerce. Even if you don't buy anything the architecture alone in the
Galleries Lafayettes is worth a visit.

A walk along the Seine and on the Île de la Cité brings you to the
Cathedral of Notre-Dame, one of the finest flowerings of French Gothic
architecture. Along with the Arc de Triomphe and the Eiffel Tower,
Notre Dame is one of the symbols of Paris. A cliché perhaps but France
coined the word cliché, and what's in a name? There are certain
clichés about a visit to Paris which are worth your while: Montmartre,
home of the Moulin Rouge whose performers and habitués became the
subject of Toulouse Lautrec's sketches and where you can still see the
can-can performed; where the gleaming Sacré-Coeur church dominates
the height; and where artists set up their easels on the street. The Eiffel
Tower is another worthwhile cliché, as is the nearby Trocadéro with its
gardens, where you might eat your lunch of French bread and paté and
cheese and watch the fountains glitter in the sun. And how about a

cruise along the river in a *bateau-mouche*, by day or night - and at night you can dine on board. Last but not least a visit to Versailles, the glorious palace of the Sun King, Louis XIV.

But it would be a mistake to make a visit to Paris one long sight-seeing trip. Better to take in some of the treasures of the city and then make it your own, to go out to Neuilly for no particular reason except to be in a Paris suburb, to go to the Bois de Boulogne simply to wander among the trees, to spend the morning sitting in cafés, go to one of the innumerable restaurants for lunch, go to the cinema, the theatre, a disco or nightclub.

Remember these things: if you like your steak medium ask for it *bien cuit*, because in France they like their meat rarer, on the whole, than the British do; and that if you go to one of the big-reputation bars the drinks may cost you more than you want to pay!

Lastly, prepare to be offended now and then by the ungiving eye of the Parisian in the street, and not to take it personally, because offence is seldom being given. It is just that to the inhabitants of the city Paris is the only place to be and they know it too. If you doubted it you would simply be asked, where else is there? So simply relax and let yourself soak up the atmosphere of romance, history, style and glamour which is Paris, City of Light.

**William Watson**

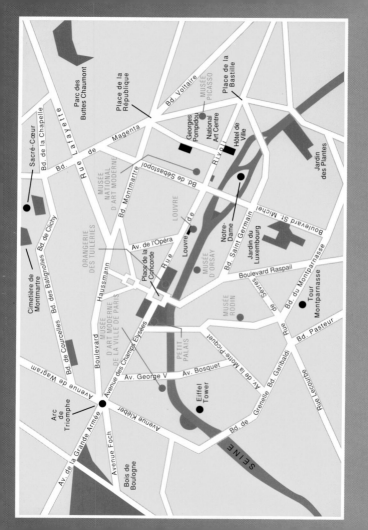

**LOUVRE** Palais du Louvre, 1er.
•0945-1700 Wed.-Mon. M Louvre, Palais-Royal •20F (free Sun.).
*One of the world's foremost collections. See* MUSEUMS 1, MUSTS, **A-Z**.

**MUSÉE NATIONAL D'ART MODERNE**
Pompidou Centre, rue Beaubourg, 4e. •1200-2200 Wed.-Mon.,
1000-2200 Sat., Sun. M Rambuteau, Hôtel de Ville. •22F.
*Impressive collection of paintings and sculptures from 1905 onwards.*

**MUSÉE D'ORSAY** 1 rue de Bellechasse, 7e.
•1000-1800 Tues.-Sun. (1000-2115 Thurs.).
M/RER Musée d'Orsay •23F (12F Sun.).
*Old Orsay station, now an art gallery for the period 1848-1914. See* **A-Z**.

**ORANGERIE DES TUILERIES** pl de la Concorde, 1e.
•0945-1715 Wed.-Mon. M Concorde. •15F.
*Impressionist and Post-Impressionist works.*

**ART MODERNE DE LA VILLE DE PARIS**
11 av du Président-Wilson, 16e.
•1000-1730 Tues.-Sun. (1000-2030 Wed.). M Iéna. •20F.
*Devoted to 20thC art, with fine examples of Cubist and Fauvist movements.*

**PETIT PALAIS** 1 av Winston-Churchill, 8e.
•1000-1745 Tues.-Sun. M Champs-Élysées-Clemenceau.
•15F (special exhibitions 25F).
*Collection of privately donated works, plus temporary exhibitions.*

**MUSÉE PICASSO** 5 rue de Thorigny, 3e.
•0915-1715 Wed.-Mon. (2000 Wed.).
M Chemin Vert, St-Paul-le-Marais. •21F.
*Superb range of Picassos, demonstrating his versatility and prolific output.*

**MUSÉE RODIN** 77 rue de Varenne, 7e.
•1000-1715 Wed.-Mon. M Varenne. •16F.
*Display of Rodin's works in the mansion where he once lived and worked.*

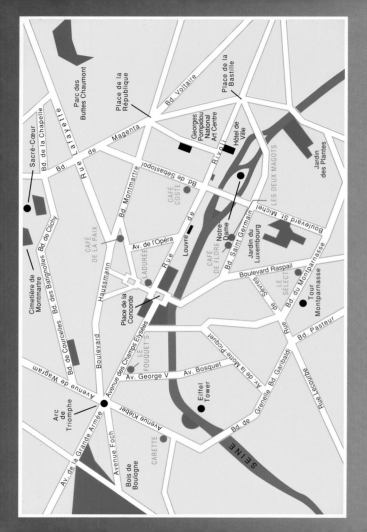

**LE FOUQUET'S** 99 av des Champs-Élysées, 8e.
•0900-2400. M Georges-V. •Coffee 20F, Carte 200F.
*A Parisian institution - the French César film awards are presented here each year. See* WALK 4.

**CAFÉ DE LA PAIX** 12 bd des Capucines, 9e.
•1200-0115. M Opéra. •Coffee 10F, Carte 150F.
*Typical pavement café, with superb Napoleon III décor.*

**LES DEUX MAGOTS** 170 bd St Germain, 6e.
•0900-2300. M St-Germain-des-Près. •Coffee 17F.
*The place for an elegant breakfast. See* WALK 3.

**CAFÉ DE FLORE** 172 bd St Germain, 6e.
•0800-2300. M St-Germain-des-Près. •Coffee 17F.
*This café is famous as the favourite haunt of literary figures 50 years ago.*

**LE SÉLECT** 99 bd du Montparnasse, 6e.
•0830-0200. M Vavin. •Coffee 10F.
*The last American bar in Montparnasse (see* CITY DISTRICTS, **Left Bank**, A-Z*) where intellectuals still congregate.*

**CAFÉ COSTES** pl des Innocents, 1er.
•0830-0200. M Les Halles, RER Châtelet-les-Halles. •Expensive.
*Ultra-chic café-bar with interior designed by Philippe Starck. Check out the toilets!*

**LADURÉE** 16 rue Royale, 8e.
•0830-1900 Mon.-Sat. Lunch 1130-1500. M Madeleine.
•Tea 23F, Coffee 14F, Cakes 17-23F, Lunch 60-80F (Plat du jour).
*Spoil yourself with the delicious variety of cakes and wide selection of teas.*

**CARETT** 4 pl du Trocadéro, 16e.
•0800-2000 daily. M Trocadéro. •Coffee 20F.
*The ultimate Paris tearoom, a good place to sit and relax after climbing the Eiffel Tower (see* MUSTS, A-Z*).*

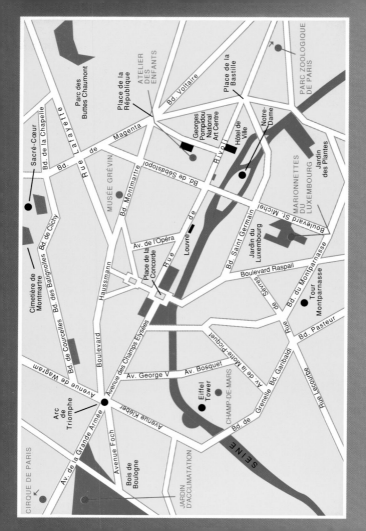

**PARC ZOOLOGIQUE DE PARIS** 53 av de St Maurice, 12e.
•0900-1800 (1700 winter). M Porte Dorée. •30F.
*Over 200 species - don't miss the lemur house. See* **Bois de Vincennes**.

**ATELIER DES ENFANTS** Pompidou Centre, Beaubourg, 4e.
•1000-1130, 1400-1530, 1545-1700 Wed; 1400-1530, 1545-1700 Sat.
M Rambuteau, Hôtel de Ville, RER Châtelet-les-Halles. •Free.
*Creative workshop for children aged five and over.*

**JARDIN D'ACCLIMATATION** Bois de Boulogne, 16e.
•1000-1800 daily. M Les Sablons. •6,80F.
*Enormous park providing playgrounds, miniature railway, go-karts,
enchanted river, zoo. See* **Bois de Boulogne**.

**MARIONNETTES DU LUXEMBOURG**
Jardin du Luxembourg, 6e.
•1500 & 1600 Sat, 1400 & 1630 Sun. M Vavin. •16F.
*Puppet show with extensive repertoire. Very popular.*

**CHAMP-DE-MARS** Champ-de-Mars, 7e.
•Open all the time. M La Motte-Picquet Grenelle, École Militaire.
•Free.
*Park next to the Eiffel Tower (see* **MUSTS**, **A-Z**), *with pony-rides, puppet
theatre and picnic areas.*

**MUSÉE GREVIN** 10 bd Montmartre, 9e.
•1300-1900 daily (1000-1900 in school holidays).
M Rue Montmartre. •38F, child 26F.
*Waxworks museum founded in 1882. Contains displays depicting episodes
from French history.*

**CIRQUE DE PARIS** av de la Commune-de-Paris, Nanterre.
•1500 Wed. & Sun. (daily during school holidays).
RER Nanterre-Ville. •45F-110F, child 35F-85F.
*A traditional circus with clowns, acrobats, magicians, jugglers, and all the
fun of the fair.*

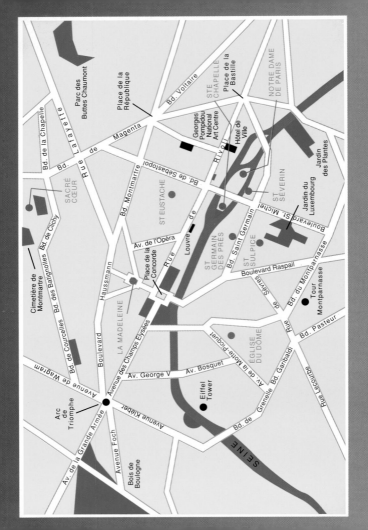

**NOTRE DAME DE PARIS** pl du Parvis Notre Dame, 4e.
•0800-1900 daily. M Cité. •Free.
*Famous masterpiece of Gothic architecture. See* **MUSTS, WALK 1, A-Z.**

**SACRÉ-COEUR** 36 rue du Chevalier de la Barre, 18e.
•0600-2300 daily. M Anvers, Abbesses. •Free.
*Its prominent white domes are one of the city's most familiar landmarks. See* **WALK 5, Montmartre, A-Z.**

**STE CHAPELLE** bd du Palais, 1er.
•1000-1620 daily. M Cité. •30F incl. entry to Conciergerie.
*Best known for its superb stained-glass windows. See* **WALK 1, A-Z.**

**LA MADELEINE** pl de la Madeleine, 8e.
•0800-1800 daily. M Madeleine. •Free.
*Built for Napoleon (see* **A-Z***) in the style of a Roman temple. See* **WALK 4.**

**ST SULPICE** pl St-Sulpice, 6e.
•0730-1700 daily. M St-Sulpice, Mabillon. •Free.
*Famous for its music: frequent recitals on Europe's largest organ. See* **A-Z.**

**ST SÉVERIN** 1 rue des Prêtres-Saint-Séverin, 5e.
•1100-1930 Mon.-Sat., 0900-2000 Sun. M/RER St-Michel.
*University church, late Gothic with modern stained glass.*

**ST-GERMAIN-DES-PRÉS** pl St-Germain-des-Prés, 6e.
•0745-1930 daily. M St-Germain-des-Prés. •Free.
*Oldest church in Paris (10th-12thC) - splendid concerts. See* **WALK 3, A-Z.**

**DÔME DES INVALIDES** av de Tourville, 7e.
•0900-1800 daily. M École-Militaire, Varennes, Invalides. •Free.
*Impressive church with magnificent dome and tomb of Napoleon. See* **A-Z.**

**ST EUSTACHE** pl du Jour, 1er.
•0830-1900 daily. M Les Halles, RER Châtelet-les-Halles. •Free.
*Laid out in Gothic style with Renaissance decoration. Exceptional concerts.*

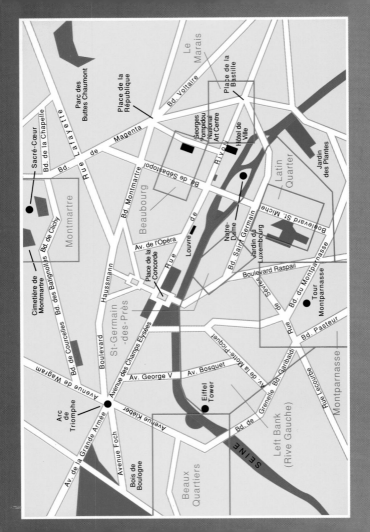

**BEAUBOURG** RER Châtelet-les-Halles.
*1er, between Les Halles and rue Beaubourg. Home of the Pompidou Centre (see A-Z) and a popular shopping area, with trendy cafés and bars.*

**BEAUX QUARTIERS** M Église d'Auteuil, Trocadéro.
*16e and southern 17e arrondissements (see A-Z). A wealthy area next to the Bois de Boulogne (see A-Z). To the north is av Foch - Paris's equivalent of Sloane Square; to the south are the village-like areas of Auteuil and Passy.*

**LE MARAIS** M Hôtel de Ville, St-Paul-le-Marais, Bastille.
*3e and 4e, between Beaubourg and pl de la Bastille (see A-Z). Originally aristocratic, now has museums, libraries and smart apartments. See WALK 2.*

**LEFT BANK (RIVE GAUCHE)** M Odéon, RER St-Michel.
*5e and 6e. South of the Seine (see A-Z), traditionally the haunt of intellectuals, students and bohemians. See MUSTS, WALK 3, A-Z.*

**MONTMARTRE** M Anvers, Abbesses, Lamarck-Caulaincourt.
*18e. On a steep hill topped by the Sacré-Coeur (see CHURCHES, A-Z). Its narrow streets which once attracted famous artists and writers are now very touristy. See MUSTS, WALK 5, A-Z.*

**MONTPARNASSE** M Montparnasse-Bienvenüe, Raspail.
*6e, 14e and 15e. Similar creative associations to Montmartre, especially between the wars. Nowadays dominated by Maine-Montparnasse complex and Tour Montparnasse. See Left Bank, A-Z.*

**LATIN QUARTER** M Odéon, RER St-Michel.
*5e. The spirit of the Left Bank is most prevalent in the narrow streets by the bd St-Michel. Pl St-Michel is always popular with tourists and students, and there are many cheaper hotels and restaurants. See WALK 3, A-Z.*

**ST-GERMAIN-DES-PRÉS** M St-Germain-des-Prés, Mabillon.
*Northern part of 6e arrondissement, around pl St-Germain-des-Prés. An attractive and lively area, slightly more up-market than the nearby Latin Quarter, with bookshops, galleries and antique shops good for a browse.*

Montmartre

Centre Georges-Pompidou

PRODUITS
DE
LA MER

CUISINES
ET
VINS

## North

**BASILIQUE DE ST DENIS** pl de l'Hôtel de Ville, St-Denis.
•1000-1800 daily. M St- Denis. •Free.
*A landmark in French architecture. See* **St-Denis Basilica**.

**ENGHIEN-LES-BAINS**
10 km north of Paris. SNCF Gare du Nord to Enghien.
*This charming town is the nearest waterside resort to Paris. The picturesque lakeside views, boating, games, festivities and the casino make it a firm favourite with the Parisians.*

**ABBAYE DE ROYAUMONT** Asnières-sur-Oise, Luzarches.
•1000-1200, 1400-1745 Wed.-Mon. (1800 Sat.-Sun.). 30 km north of Paris. SNCF Gare du Nord to Luzarches. Car - A1 north then C909 at La Croix Verte. •16F, under 16s, students and OAPs 10F.
*Cistercian abbey founded in 1228 by Louis IX, of majestic dimensions but beautiful simplicity. Do not miss the refectory - a masterpiece of Gothic art.*

**CHANTILLY** Musée Condé and Château.
•1000-1800 Wed.-Mon. 45 km north on A1 (turn off at Survilliers). SNCF: Gare du Nord to Chantilly. •30F, under 12s 7F. (park only 12F, child 7F).
*The Château de Chantilly stands on a splendid carp-filled lake, and houses the Musée Condé. See* **A-Z**.

**SENLIS** pl du Parvis Notre Dame.
SNCF Gare du Nord to Chantilly, then bus to Senlis.
*The cathedral, built 1155-1184, is contemporary with St Denis (see* **A-Z***) and Notre Dame (see* **CHURCHES, MUSTS, WALK 1, A-Z***).*

**PARC ASTÉRIX PLAILLY** Oise-en-Picardie.
•1000-1900 daily. 38 km north of Paris on A1. SNCF Gare du Nord to Fosses. •120F, 3-12 years 90F.
*Adventure park created along the theme of the well-known comic-strip character. Five main areas - Asterix's World, Rome, Imaginary World, Lake and the Paris street (outlining the history of France) - featuring shows, games, exhibitions, restaurants and shop.*

## ST-GERMAIN-EN-LAYE
•0945-1200, 1330-1715 Wed.-Mon. RER Line A1. •15F, under 24s 8F.
*Renaissance castle and Museum of National Antiquities. See **A-Z**.*

## ST-CLOUD Parc de Le Nôtre.
•0700-2200 daily. M Boulogne-Pont de St-Cloud.
*Park designed by Le Nôtre, with fine views overlooking the Seine (see **A-Z**).*

## SÈVRES Musée National de la Céramique.
•1000-1200, 1330-1715 Wed.-Mon. M Pont de Sèvres. •15F (8F Sun.).
*Displays of porcelain from all over the world.*

## MEUDON SNCF Montparnasse to Versailles Rive-Gauche.
Musée d'Art et d'Histoire, 11 rue des Pierres.
•1400-1800 Wed.-Sun. •Free.
Musée National Auguste Rodin, 19 av Auguste-Rodin.
•1330-1800 Sat.-Mon. •8F (Under 18s free, 18-25 and OAPs 4F).
*Two interesting museums: one covers local history with a section on abstract art from the 1950s and 60s; the other is Rodin's former residence where you can see sketches, plaster models of sculptures and his tomb.*

## MARLY Musée-Promenade de Marly-le-Roi.
Car - A13 towards St-Germain-en-Laye. SNCF St Lazare-St-Nom-la-Bretèche. •1400-1800 Wed.-Sun. •10F, under 18s 5F, under 8s free.
*The museum pays tribute to the artistic and literary life of the 19thC, including the Impressionists, who were particularly fond of the grounds.*

## THOIRY Château and parc Zoologique, Thoiry-en-Yvelines.
40 km west on A13. SNCF Montparnasse to Montfort L'Amaury (Dreux train) or Villiers, RER line C5 to Versailles Rive-Gauche.
•1000-1800 Mon.-Sat., 1000-1830 Sun. •59F adult, 49F child for zoo, gardens and African reserve; 80F (71F) with castle.
*A 16thC castle housing an archive and gastronomy museum. The grounds have been converted into an animal park, boasting 800 animals at liberty including an African reserve (visit by minibus) and beautifully laid-out botanical gardens (Le Nôtre, English). Also playground and restaurants.*

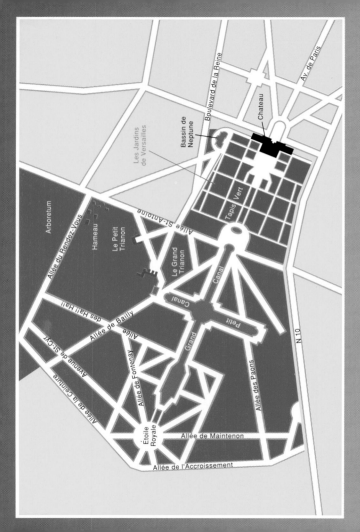

## Versailles

*22 km west of Paris.*
*RER line C to Versailles Rive-Gauche, or train from SNCF Gare Invalides,*
*St-Lazare or Montparnasse. Bus 171 from M Pont de Sèvres. Car - A 13.*
*•Castle 0945-1700 Tues.-Sun. •23F, reduced rate 12F.*

The main attraction of Versailles (see **A-Z**) is the world-famous 17thC castle and gardens which housed the French Court and Government from 1682 to the French Revolution. Originally a small hunting lodge, the building was rebuilt and greatly extended between 1661-1720 to become the royal seat of Louis XIV. During the Revolutionary period it was abandoned, then later made into a museum in 1830. A visit should include the State Apartments, Hall of Mirrors, Queen's Apartment, Chapel and the historical museum. The King's Suite, Royal Opera and King's Private Apartments can only be visited by guided tour (various conducted tours are available on Tuesday and Friday afternoons at an additional cost of 15F an hour).

**Les Jardins de Versailles** - Laid out by Le Nôtre along two axes, these gardens are a masterpiece of elegance and formality. After visiting the Bassin de Neptune, the most impressive of the gardens, and admiring the view from the central steps, stroll down the Tapis Vert to examine the statues and vases that line the avenue. On your left is the Colonnade (designed by Mansart in 1685) of coloured marble, which constitutes one of the park's most beautiful ornaments. It is possible to rent bicycles and boats (45F per hr) near the Grand Canal. The *Grandes Eaux* (when you can see the fountains play) take place on Sundays at 1115 and 1530 from May to October, at a cost of 15F.

**Le Grand Trianon** - (•0945-1200, 1400-1700. •15F, reduced rate 8F.) A small pink marble and stone castle built for Louis XIV by Mansart. This is where the king entertained his intimate friends, Madame de Maintenon in particular. Do not miss the gallery which displays some illustrations of the gardens of Versailles and Trianon.

**Le Petit Trianon** - (•1400-1700. •10F, reduced rate 5F) was a great favourite of Marie-Antoinette's. Its most interesting feature is the Guibert panelling throughout the first floor apartments. The gardens are in Anglo-Chinese style and lead to the **Hameau** - ten thatched cottages where the queen liked to indulge her rustic fantasies.

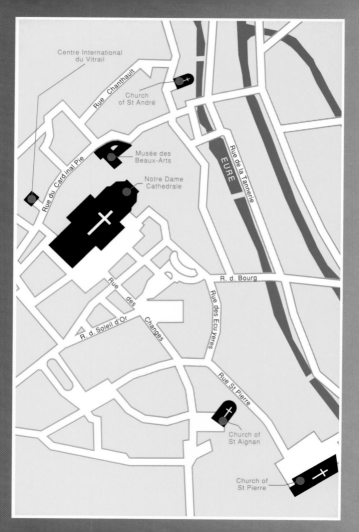

Centre International
du Vitrail

Rue Chanthault

Church
of St André

Rue du Card inal Pie

Musée des
Beaux-Arts

Notre Dame
Cathedrale

Rue de la Tannerie

EURE

R. d. Bourg

Rue des Changes

Rue des Ecuyeres

R. d. Solell d'Or

Rue St Pierre

Church of
St Aignan

Church of
St Pierre

## Chartres

*90 km south of Paris.*
*SNCF Gare Montparnasse. Car - A11 (Paris-Le Mans), A10 (Paris-Bordeaux),*
*RN10 (Paris-Hendaye).*

Although Chartres is best known for its cathedral the town has many
other buildings of historical and architectural interest and offers a
charming day out from Paris. Easily accessible by train, from the station
follow the signs towards the town centre, keeping the cathedral's twin
towers in view. The friendly staff of the tourist office (Parvis de la
Cathédrale, BP 289, 28005 Chartres. •0930-1230, 1400-1830; Sun. in
summer 1000-1200, 1500-1800) will help you plan your day. You can
hire a walkman with two headphones for 35F which takes you through
an hour-long self-guided tour of the old town. Otherwise, you can simply follow the signs marked '*Circuit Touristique*'. An alternative is a trip
on the small tourist train which leaves from the place de la Cathédrale
every 35-40 minutes (•1000-1900 daily Apr.-Nov. •20F, child 10F).
Buildings of interest include:

**Notre Dame Cathedrale -** (•0730-1900 daily). This magnificent 13thC
High Gothic building dominates the whole town. Erected on the site of
an 11thC crypt, it has been a popular place of pilgrimage since the
Middle Ages. It is of elegant and majestic dimensions and boasts a
unique collection of stained glass windows covering several centuries
and various themes. The treasury (• 1000-1200, 1400-1800) houses the
'Veil of the Virgin Mary' donated by Charles the Bald in 876. The exterior, with its green copper roof (which replaced the original structure
after a fire in 1836), bears two asymmetric towers - the old bell-tower
(south) and the intricately worked new bell-tower (north). Guided tours
in English are available at 1215 daily or contact Mr Malcolm Miller (26
rue des Ecuyers, tel 37.28.15.58) to book group tours (400F an hour).

**Centre International du Vitrail -** (•1000-1230, 1300-1800 Tues.-Sun.
•12F). It is less well known that Chartres is an international stained-
glass centre and has over 2500 m² of windows throughout its churches.
Housed in a fine, half-timbered medieval corn loft, the International
Centre of Stained-Glass Art runs exhibitions of contemporary artists
from all over the world. Underground is the beautiful rib-vaulted,
triple-naved Cellier de Loens which is used for social functions.

Chartres

**Musée des Beaux-Arts** - (•1000-1200, 1400-1800 Wed.-Mon. in summer and until 1700 in winter. •6F). The museum contains 16th and 18thC tapestries, an important collection of medieval polychrome wood sculptures, 16th-19thC paintings and some interesting 12th and 13thC harpsichords and spinets. It is housed in the former bishop's beautiful palace, the construction of which spanned four centuries (15th to 18th). There is a stunning view over the old town and down to the river Eure from the terraced gardens.

**Church of St Pierre** - Founded in the 7thC, it served as the abbey church for the Benedictine monks. The interior is extremely simple and enhanced by the splendour of its late 13th/early 14thC stained-glass windows which occupy the whole of the upper floor.

**Church of St André -** On the banks of the river Eure, this former 12thC Romanesque church was restored in 1960 after being partially destroyed by a fire in 1944. The choir used to be on an arch, the remains of which can still be seen, across the river. Today it is used for video shows and lectures on local history.

**Church of St Aignan** - Rebuilt in the 16thC after being damaged by fire, the church shows features of the Renaissance style, especially in the elaborate stained-glass windows of the south side.


**RAMBOUILLET** Château de Rambouillet.
•1000-1200, 1400-1800 Wed.-Mon. SNCF Gare Montparnasse.
•22F, child 5F.
The castle of Rambouillet is set in the heart of 20,000 hectares of woodland called the Yvelines forest. It was almost completely rebuilt in the 18thC in keeping with medieval style, and all that is left of the original 14thC structure is the round tower of the keep. Once used by numerous kings of France as a hunting residence, it still serves as an official residence of the President. You can visit the charming *boudoir* of Marie-Antoinette and the private quarters of Napoleon I (see **A-Z**). In the grounds, the exterior of a seemingly simple thatched building belies an interior elaborately decorated in shells, marble and mother-of-pearl. King Louis XVI's present to Marie-Antoinette, an exquisite little dairy, can also be visited.

## Fontainebleau

*65 km from Paris.*
*SNCF Gare de Lyon then bus from Fontainebleau station. Car - N7 from the*
*Porte d'Italie.*

Fontainebleau is a favourite weekend retreat for Parisians attracted by
the vast 20,000 hectare forest and 16thC castle. Visits to the forest are
unfortunately limited to those who have their own cars though it is possible to hire bicycles at the station (•40F per day, 30F for half a day). If
you enjoy walking, maps of suggested itineraries can be obtained from
the tourist office (31 pl Napoleon Bonaparte, opposite the post office).
**Château de Fontainebleau** - (•0930-1230, 1400-1700 Wed.-Mon.
Grands Appartements and Musée Napoléon I - •23F, 18-25 years and
OAPs 12F; Petits Appartements 10F).
Although it dates back to the 12thC, it was François I who was respon-
sible for the castle as we know it today, with its ensemble of 16thC
buildings and collection of Italian Renaissance art. As you enter the
grounds into the Cour des Adieux where Napoleon I (see **A-Z**) bade
farewell to his Imperial Guard after his abdication in 1814, you will see
the well-known horseshoe staircase in front of you (Ducerceau, 1634).
This leads to the former entrance of the medieval castle on the first
floor. A stroll round the Grands Appartements (about 45 min) takes you
through the Gallery of François I, where you can admire the delicate
frescoes by Le Rosso, before going up the Escalier d'Honneur into the
splendid ballroom decorated with frescoes by N. dell'Abbate.
Other rooms on the first floor include the apartments of Madame de
Maintenon, Marie-Antoinette and those of Napoleon I, which overlook
the Jardins de Diane. Of particular interest are the regal Throne Room,
which was the only one existing outside Versailles, and the beautiful
Salle du Conseil which is a fine example of 18thC decor. In the
Chapelle de la Trinite are some paintings by Freminet. The Petits
Appartements (guided tour only) reveal Louis Quinze-style decoration
and Empire furniture, and the Galerie des Cerfs with wall paintings
depicting royal hunts. To the right of the Cour des Adieux, a passage
leads to the Cour de la Fontaine which is bordered by a pond filled
with carp, some of which are enormous. Go through the Porte Dorée
(Golden Gate) to the square terrace for a superb view of the grounds.

Versailles

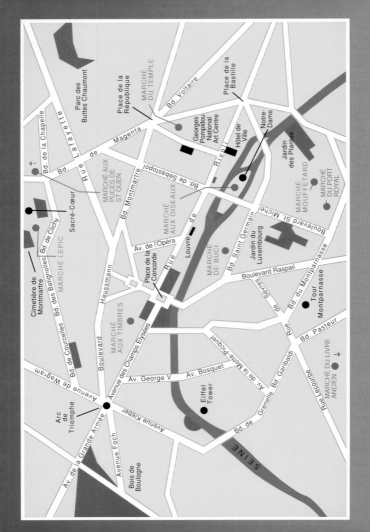

### MARCHÉ AUX OISEAUX  pl Louis-Lépine, 4e.
•0900-1700 daily. M Cité.
*Bird and flower market, well worth a visit.*

### MARCHÉ AUX PUCES DE ST OUEN  Porte de Clignancourt,.
•0500-1800 Sat.-Mon. M Porte de St-Ouen, Porte de Clignancourt.
*Eight separate markets, each with its own specialities and reputation.*

### MARCHÉ DU LIVRE ANCIEN
Pavillon de Baltard, Parc Georges Brassens, 15e.
•0800-1800 Sat., Sun. M Porte de Vanves.
*Unique in Paris and situated at the old Vaugirard horse market.*

### MARCHÉ DE BUCI  rue de Buci, 6e.
•0800-1800 Tues.-Sun. M Odéon.
*Bustling food and flower market.*

### MARCHÉ AUX TIMBRES  av Matignon, av Gabriel, 8e.
•0800-1800 Thurs., Sat., Sun. M Franklin-D-Roosevelt.
*Stamp and postcard market - a mecca for enthusiasts. See* **WALK 4**.

### MARCHÉ DU PORT ROYAL  bd de Port-Royal, 5e.
•0700-1300 Tues., Thurs., Sat. M Port-Royal.
*Open-air food market, one of 57 in Paris.*

### MARCHÉ MOUFFETARD  rue Mouffetard, 5e.
•0700-1300 Tues.-Sun. M Censier-Daubenton.
*Typical Parisian food market, colourful with intriguing aromas. See* **A-Z**.

### MARCHÉ LEPIC  rue Lepic, 18e.
•0800-1400 Tues.-Sun. M Blanche.
*Food market, renowned for fresh produce.*

### MARCHÉ DE TEMPLE  rue Perrée, 3e.
•0900-1200 Tues.-Sun. M Temple.
*The Carreau du Temple is a very old covered market specializing in clothes.*

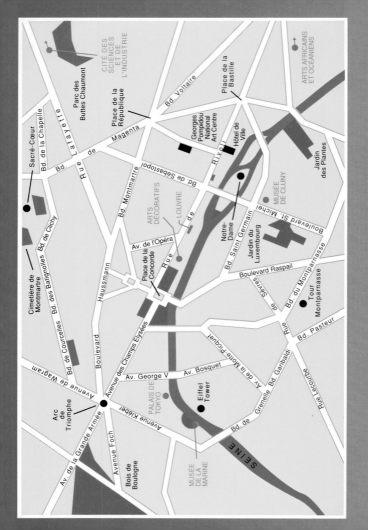

**MUSÉE DU LOUVRE** Palais du Louvre, 1er.
•0945-1700,1830 Wed.-Mon. M Louvre, Palais-Royal.
•25F (free Sun.).
*The most famous museum in Paris. Home of the* Mona Lisa *(see* **A-Z***) and the* Venus de Milo. *See* ART GALLERIES, MUSTS, **A-Z**.

**CITÉ DES SCIENCES ET DE L'INDUSTRIE**
30 av Corentin-Cariou, 19e.
•0900-1900 Tues.-Sun. M Porte de la Villette. •30F.
*A showcase of science and technology, situated in La Villette Park.*

**ARTS DÉCORATIFS** 107 rue de Rivoli, 1er.
•1230-1800 Wed.-Sun. M Palais-Royal, Tuileries. •20F.
*Traces the development of the decorative arts.*

**PALAIS DE TOKYO** 13 av du Président-Wilson, 16e.
•0945-1715 Wed.-Mon. M Iéna. •25F.
*The National Photography Centre, with exhibitions of both historical and contemporary photographs.*

**MUSÉE DE CLUNY** 6 pl Paul-Painlevé, 5e.
•0945-1230, 1400-1715 Wed.-Mon. M Odéon.
•15F (8F Sun.).
*Medieval arts and crafts, including the* Lady with the Unicorn *tapestry.*

**ARTS AFRICAINS ET OCÉANIENS** 293 av Damesnil, 12e.
•1000-1200 Mon.-Fri., 1000-1800 Sat., Sun.
M Porte Dorée. •22F (13F Sun.).
*Arts and crafts from Africa, the Pacific and Australia, plus an enormous tropical aquarium.*

**MUSÉE DE LA MARINE**
Palais de Chaillot, pl du Trocadero, 16e.
•1000-1800 Wed.-Mon. M Trocadéro. •18F.
*Naval museum with a superb collection of rare model ships, paintings and engravings.*

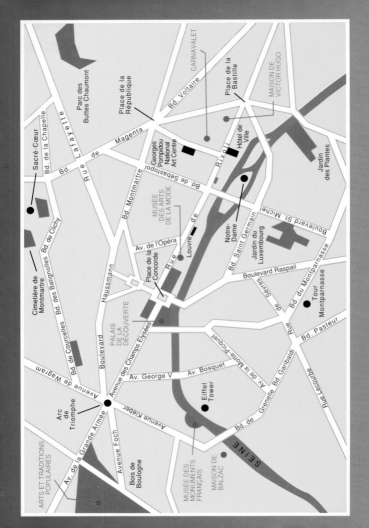

## MUSÉE DES MONUMENTS FRANÇAIS
Palais de Chaillot, pl du Trocadéro, 16e.
•0945-1230, 1400-1715 Wed.-Mon. M Trocadéro. •15F (8F Sun.).
*Museum of monumental art and murals, based on an idea by Viollet le Duc.*

## MUSÉE DES ARTS DE LA MODE 109 rue de Rivoli, 1er.
•1230-1830 Wed.-Sat., 1100-1800 Sun.
M Palais-Royal, Tuileries. •20F.
*Also known as Pavillon de Marsan, this museum traces the history of Haute Couture and displays creations by Chanel, Dior, Yves St Laurent and many other great fashion designers.*

## MAISON DE VICTOR HUGO 6 pl des Vosges, 4e.
•1000-1710 Tues.-Sun. M St-Paul-le-Marais, Chemin-vert. •15F.
*16thC residence displaying collections of Hugo's personal souvenirs, books and illustrations of his works. See* **WALK 2.**

## MAISON DE BALZAC 47 rue Raynouard, 16e.
•1000-1740 Tues.-Sun. M Passy. •12F.
*The home of the great novelist Honoré de Balzac from 1840-47.*

## ARTS ET TRADITIONS POPULAIRES
6 av du Mahatma Ghandi, 16e.
•1000-1715 Wed.-Mon. M Les Sablons. •14F.
*Folk museum depicting everyday life in pre-industrial France.*

## PALAIS DE LA DÉCOUVERTE av Franklin-D-Roosevelt, 8e.
•1000-1800 Tues.-Sun. M Franklin-D-Roosevelt.
•15F (plus 11F for planetarium).
*Fascinating educational exhibits illustrating and explaining some of the great discoveries in the sciences.*

## CARNAVALET 23 rue de Sévigné, 3e.
•1000-1740 Tues.-Sun. M St Paul. •20F (free Sun.).
*A splendid 17thC house with exhibits which reflect the history of Paris through the centuries. See* **WALK 2.**

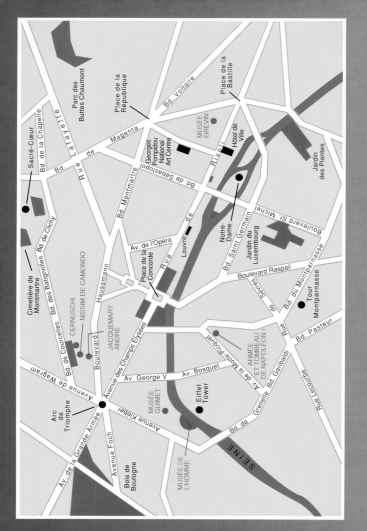

**JACQUEMART ANDRÉ** 158 bd Haussmann, 8e.
•1100-1800 Wed.-Mon. M St-Philippe-du-Roule. •25F.
*First-rate collection of 18thC European and Italian Renaissance work
displayed in a 19thC house.*

**NISSIM DE CAMONDO** 63 rue de Monceau, 8e.
•1000-1200, 1400-1700 Wed.-Sun. M Monceau, Villiers. •15F.
*Built as a replica of a luxurious 18thC private residence and filled with
furniture and objets d'art.*

**CERNUSCHI** 7 av Velasquez, 8e.
•1000-1740 Tues.-Sun. M Villiers. •15F.
*Collection devoted to ancient Chinese art, with especially fine chinaware.*

**ARMÉE ET TOMBEAU DE NAPOLÉON I**
Hôtel des Invalides, 7e.
•1000-1700 Wed.-Mon. M Latour-Maubourg. •23F.
*Weapons, uniforms and historical relics, including some which belonged to
Napoleon (see A-Z).*

**MUSÉE GREVIN** Forum des Halles, 1er.
•1030-1930 Mon.-Sat., 1300-2000 Sun.
RER Châtelet-les-Halles.•34F, child 6-14yrs 22F.
*The characters and atmosphere of turn-of-the-century Paris are recreated in
this waxwork museum.*

**MUSÉE DE L'HOMME** Palais de Chaillot, pl du Trocadéro, 16e.
•0945-1715 Wed.-Mon. M Trocadéro.
•16F (special exhibitions 16F, or 25F for both).
*Biological, anthropological and historical displays exploring the origins,
development and progress of various cultures worldwide.*

**MUSÉE GUIMET** 6 pl d'Iéna, 16e.
•0945-1715 Wed.-Mon. M Iéna. •16F.
*Beautifully displayed selection of Asian and Oriental works of art, including
statues and ceramics.*

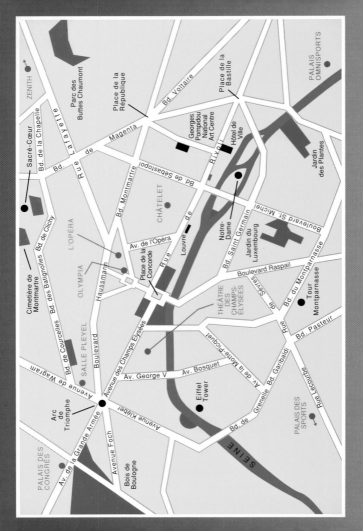

**L'OPÉRA** pl de l'Opéra, 9e.
•Box office 1100-2000, visits 1100-1700. M Opéra. •30F-300F.
*World's largest opera house, the Palais Garnier See* **WALK 4**, **A-Z**.

**PALAIS OMNISPORTS** 8 bd de Bercy, 12e.
•See programme for times and costs. M Bercy, Quai de la Gare.
*Multi-purpose venue hosting opera, rock concerts, cycle-races, ice-hockey.*

**THÉÂTRE DES CHAMPS-ÉLYSÉES** 15 av Montaigne, 8e.
•See programme for times. M Alma Marceau. •40F-300F.
*1912 theatre, has been played by the Marquis de Cuevas and Louis Jouvet.*

**SALLE PLEYEL** 252 rue du Faubourg-St-Honoré, 8e.
•See programme for times. M Ternes. •50F-350F.
*Home of the Orchestre de Paris, a shrine for classical music lovers.*

**CHÂTELET** pl du Châtelet, 1er.
•See programme for times and costs. RER Châtelet-les-Halles.
*Presents light opera, concerts, ballets and a few musical comedies.*

**PALAIS DES SPORTS** Porte de Versailles, 15e.
•See programme for times and costs. M Porte de Versailles.
*Enormous '60s auditorium, ideal for great events, eg 'Holiday on Ice'.*

**ZÉNITH** 211 av Jean-Jaurès, 19e.
•See programme for times and costs. M Porte de Pantin.
*A massive 'inflatable' venue for rock and pop concerts.*

**PALAIS DES CONGRÈS** Porte Maillot, 17e.
•See programme for times and costs. M Porte Maillot.
*In the Centre des Congrès, this large auditorium is used for shows as well as conferences.*

**OLYMPIA** 28 bd des Capucines, 9e.
•Box office 1000-1900 Mon.-Sat. M Opéra, Madeleine.•100F-220F.
*Most famous music hall in Paris, host to French and international stars.*

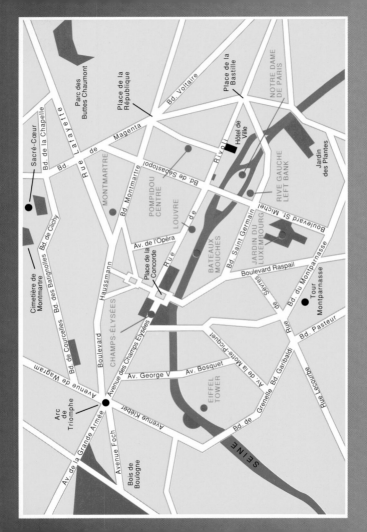

# MUSTS

## BATEAUX MOUCHES
*Glass-topped cruise boats which carry tourists up and down the river (see* **Seine***). The floodlit evening trips are particularly enjoyable. See* **A-Z**.

## CHAMPS-ÉLYSÉES
*Famous, historical avenue - wonderful for a stroll, and a coffee at Le Fouquet's (see* **CAFÉS***). See* **WALK 4***,* **A-Z**.

## EIFFEL TOWER
*Not to be missed, Gustave Eiffel's world-famous tower with tremendous views over the city. See* **A-Z**.

## LEFT BANK
*Bustling streets with fascinating bookshops, lots of students and cobbled quays by the Seine (see* **A-Z***). See* **CITY DISTRICTS***,* **WALK 3***,* **A-Z**.

## LOUVRE
*Probably the most important art collection in the world, including the Mona Lisa (see* **A-Z***) and the Venus de Milo. See* **ART GALLERIES***,* **MUSEUMS 1***,* **A-Z**.

## MONTMARTRE
*Funicular railway travels to the top of Montmartre with incredible views over Paris. See* **CITY DISTRICTS***,* **WALK 5***,* **A-Z**.

## NOTRE DAME DE PARIS
*The Cathedral church of Paris and an outstanding example of French art and architecture. The rose windows, soaring buttresses and west facade are particularly noteworthy. See* **CHURCHES***,* **WALK 1***,* **A-Z**.

## POMPIDOU CENTRE
*Multi-cultural centre, built to a controversial design. Enjoy the street entertainers outside. See* **ART GALLERIES***,* **A-Z**.

## JARDIN DU LUXEMBOURG
*Stroll among the lovers, the students studying in the sun, children playing; watch a game of boules, sit and watch Paris relaxing. See* **PARKS***,* **A-Z**.

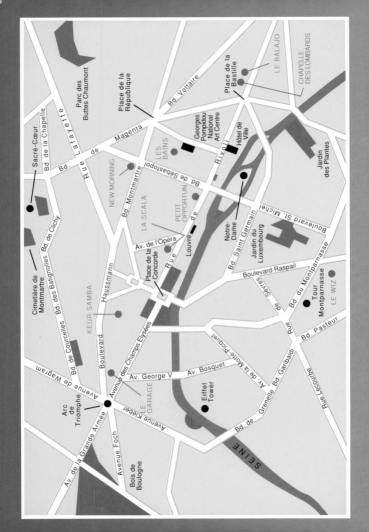

**CHAPELLE DES LOMBARDS** 19 rue de Lappe, 11e.
•2220-dawn Tues.-Sat. M Bastille. •70F, incl. first drink.
*Selection of salsa, reggae and the blues with live bands Thurs.-Sat.*

**NEW MORNING** 7-9 rue des Petites Écuries, 9e.
•2100-0130. Concerts start 2200. M Chateau d'Eau. •110F entry.
*Spacious, comfortable venue for big-name jazz bands and musicians.*

**PETIT OPPORTUN** 15 rue des Lavandieres-Ste-Opportune, 1er.
•2300-0300 Wed.-Mon. RER Châtelet-les-Halles.
•100F first drink, then 50F.
*Great place for well-known jazz musicians, especially Americans.*

**LES BAINS** 7 rue du Bourg-l'Abbé, 3e.
•2300-0600. M Étienne-Marcel. •80F, incl. first drink.
*Extremely trendy nightspot in an old Turkish bath-house.*

**LA SCALA** 188 rue de Rivoli, 1er.
•2230-dawn. M Tuileries, Palais-Royal. •90F, incl. first drink.
*Very large, with five bars and three dance floors. Popular and crowded.*

**LE BALAJO** 9 rue de Lappe, 11e.
•2200-0430 Mon., Fri., Sat. M Bastille. •80F, incl. first drink.
*Varied entertainment, with disco on Mon., ballroom dancing at weekends.*

**LE GARAGE** 41 rue Washington, 8e.
•2300-dawn. M George-V. •110F incl. first drink.
*Disco with Funk music, popular with young clientele.*

**KEUR SAMBA** 79 rue de la Boétie, 8e.
•2300-dawn. M Miromesnil, St-Phillipe-du-Roule. •70F incl. first drink.
*Extremely popular. West Indian music.*

**LE WIZ** 20 rue de la Gaîté, 14e.
•2300-dawn. M Edgar-Quinet. •50F weekdays (with drink); 80F Sat.
*Hollywood-style disco, largest in the world.*

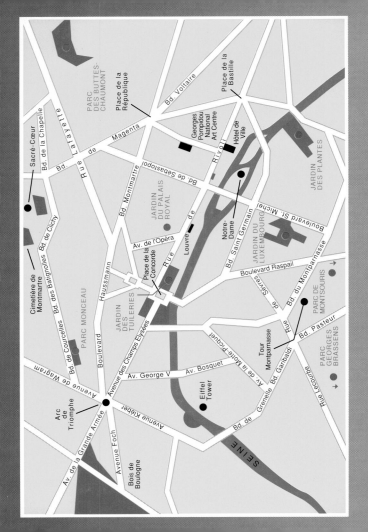

**JARDIN DES PLANTES** 57 rue Cuvier, 5e.
•0715-dusk (summer), 0800-dusk (winter). M Jussieu.
•Gardens free; menagerie 20F.
*Extensive botanical gardens with 10,000 different species of plants.
There is also a small zoo and natural history museum.*

**JARDIN DES TUILERIES** 1er.
•0800-2000. M Tuileries, Concorde. •Free.
*Gardens designed by the notable landscape gardener, Le Nôtre, on the right
bank of the Seine (see **A-Z**).*

**JARDIN DU LUXEMBOURG** 6e.
•0730-nightfall. RER Luxembourg. •Free.
*Gardens of the Senate House, with tennis courts, croquet lawns, children's
playground, café, fountains, formal vistas, sunbathers. See **MUSTS**, **WALK 3**.*

**JARDIN DU PALAIS ROYAL** 1er.
•Open all the time. M Palais-Royal. •Free.
*Formal gardens lined by arcades with a modern sculpture by Buren.*

**PARC DES BUTTES-CHAUMONT**
rue Manin, rue de Crimée, 19e.
•0700-2300 daily. M Buttes-Chaumont, Botzaris. •Free.
*Waterfalls, lake, grottoes and view of Montmartre (see **CITY DISTRICTS**, **A-Z**).*

**PARC DE MONTSOURIS** bd Jourdan, rue Gazan, 14e.
•0800-dusk. RER Cité Universitaire. •Free.
*Site of the Municipal Observatory with splendid lake and waterfalls.*

**PARC MONCEAU** bd de Courcelles, 8e.
•Open at all times. M Courcelles, Monceau. •Free.
*18thC garden with pagodas, fake ruins, playground and roller-skating park.*

**PARC GEORGES BRASSENS** rue des Morillons, 15e.
•0800-dusk. M Convention. •Free.
*New garden in centre of the city - try to visit the aromatic herb garden.*

Bois de Boulogne

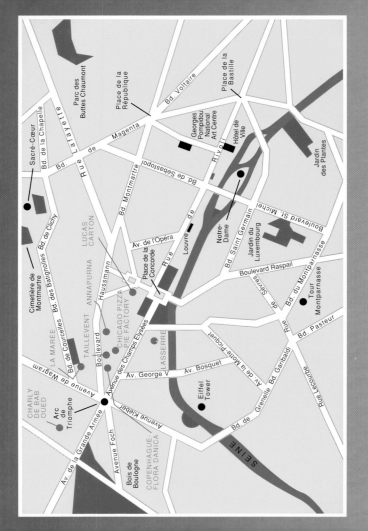

# RESTAURANTS 1

**LA MARÉE** 1 rue Daru, 8e.
•1230-1430, 2000-2230 Mon.-Fri. Closed Aug.
M Ternes, Courcelles. •400F.
*Excellent fresh seafood, simply cooked and professionally served.*

**LASSERRE** 17 av Franklin-D-Roosevelt, 8e.
•Open till 2300. Closed Sun., Mon. lunch, Aug. M Franklin-D-Roosevelt.
*World-famous; opened just after the war and retains the original decor.*

**ANNAPURNA** 32 rue de Berri, 8e.
•Open till 2330. Closed Sat. lunch, Sun. M St-Phillipe-du-Roule. •200F.
*Much respected Indian restaurant, the oldest in the city.*

**CHICAGO PIZZA PIE FACTORY** 5 rue de Berri, 8e.
•1130-2400 (0100 Fri., Sat.). M George-V. •100F.
*Place for authentic 'deep-dish' pizzas. Happy hour 1800-1930, cocktails.*

**COPENHAGUE-FLORA DANICA** 142 av des Champs-Élysées,
8e. •1200-1430, 1915-2230. Closed Sun., Aug. (Copenhague).
RER Charles-de-Gaulle, M Étoile, George-V. •200F-300F.
*Copenhague is on the first floor, the cheaper Flora Danica plus snack-bar on the ground floor.*

**CHARLY DE BAB OUED** 95 bd Gouvion-St-Cyr, 17e.
•Open till 2300. M Porte Maillot. •200F.
*Authentic Middle Eastern food served amid palms, flowers and pot-plants.*

**LUCAS CARTON** 9 pl de la Madeleine, 8e.
•Open till 2230 Mon.-Fri. Closed Aug. M Madeleine.
•500F-1000F incl. wine.
*Voted the best in Paris, 1988. Excellent cuisine in art deco surroundings.*

**TAILLEVENT** 15 rue Lammenais, 8e.
•Open till 2230 Mon.-Fri. Closed 23 July-22 Aug. M George-V.
•500F incl. wine.
*Prestigious restaurant, much admired for its nouvelle cuisine.*

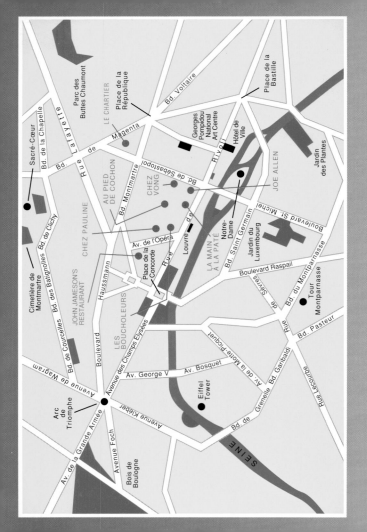

## Halles-Opéra

**LA MAIN À LA PÂTE** 35 rue St Honoré, 1er.
• 1130-0030 Mon.-Sat. RER Châtelet-les-Halles.
• 200F incl. wine.
*Adjacent to Forum des Halles, very friendly, cheerful atmosphere.*

**CHEZ VONG** 10 rue de la Grande Truanderie, 1er.
• 1230-1500, 2000-2400 Mon.-Sat. M Étienne-Marcel.
• 200F-300F.
*One of the best Chinese restaurants in Paris.*

**JOE ALLEN** 30 rue Pierre Lescot, 1er.
• 1200-0100. M Étienne-Marcel. • 150F-200F.
*Popular New York-style restaurant , serves barbecue ribs and cheesecake.*

**AU PIED DE COCHON** 6 rue Coquillière, 1er.
• Open 24 hrs. RER Chatelet-les-Halles. • 150F-200F.
*In the 'Les Halles' tradition with 19thC interior and seafood specialities.*

**CHEZ PAULINE** 5 rue Villedo, 1er.
• 1215-1430, 1930-2230. Closed Sat. evenings, Sun., July.
M Pyramides. • 200F-300F.
*Traditional French cuisine, popular with locals as well as tourists.*

**LES BOUCHOLEURS** 4 rue de Richelieu, 1er.
• Open till 2300. Closed Sat. lunch, Sun. M Palais-Royal.
• 200F.
*Small restaurant with nautical interior. Specializes in seafood.*

**JOHN JAMESONS' RESTAURANT** 10 rue des Capucines, 2e.
• 1200-1430, 1900-0030 Tues.-Sun.
M Opéra. • 150F-200F.
*Enjoy the atmosphere of old Ireland, plus Kitty O'Shea's Pub.*

**LE CHARTIER** 7 rue du Faubourg Montmartre, 9e.
• 1100-1500, 1800-2130. M Rue Montmartre. • 60F.
*The poor man's Maxim's. Superb fin de siècle setting.*

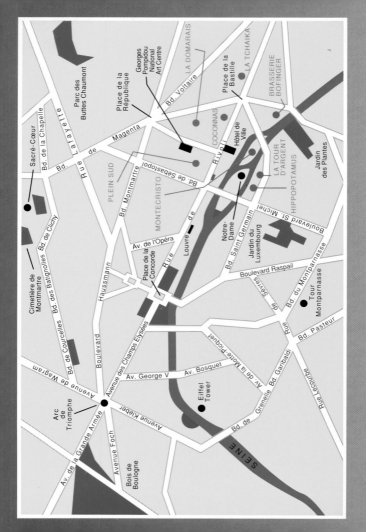

## Marais-Île St Louis

**HIPPOPOTAMUS** 6 av Franklin-D-Roosevelt, 8e.
•1130-1600, 1830-0100. M Franklin-D-Roosevelt. •150F.
*One of a chain of restaurants specializing in grilled beef dishes.*

**PLEIN SUD** 10 rue St-Merri, 4e.
•1100-2300. M Rambuteau, Hôtel de Ville. •100F.
*The explosive cocktails and enchiladas are well worth a try.*

**BRASSERIE BOFINGER** 3 rue de la Bastille, 4e.
•1200-1500, 1930-0100. M Bastille. •100F-200F.
*Established 1864, the oldest brasserie in Paris retaining 1900s décor - do try the choucroute.*

**COCONNAS** pl des Vosges, 4e.
•1215-1415, 1945-2200 Wed.-Sun. Closed mid Dec.-mid Jan.
M St-Paul-le-Marais. •150F-200F.
*Traditional French cuisine in a tavern atmosphere.*

**MONTECRISTO** 81 rue St-Louis-en-l'Ile, 4e.
•1130-2230 Mon.-Sat. Closed Aug. M Pont Marie.•150F-200F.
*An old Île-St-Louis house offering friendly service in attractive, small dining-rooms.*

**LA TCHAIKA** 7 rue de Lappe, 11e.
•1200-1500, 1930-2300 Mon.-Sat. M Bastille. •100F-150F.
*Peaceful and friendly environment: enjoy Slavonic fare in a Russian drawing-room setting.*

**LE DOMARAIS** 53 bis rue des Francs-Bourgeois, 4e.
•1130-2330. Closed Sun. & Mon. lunchtime. M Hôtel de Ville, Rambuteau.
*In the heart of the Marais, an exceptional circular dining room with cupola.*

**LA TOUR D'ARGENT** 17 quai de la Tournelle, 5e.
•1200-1400, 2000-2200 Tues.-Sun. M Maubert-Mutualité.
•500F (lunch 350F).
*Excellent food, great views of Notre Dame (see **CHURCHES**, **MUSTS**, **A-Z**).*

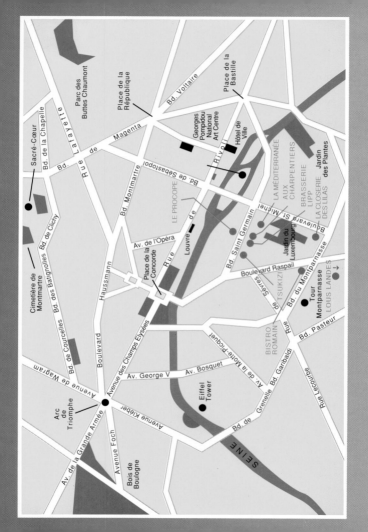

## Rive Gauche

**LOUS LANDES** 157 av du Maine, 14e.
•1200-1500, 1930-2300 Mon.-Sat. M Gaîté. •200F-250F.
*Restaurant specializing in food from south-west France: excellent* foie-gras.

**LE PROCOPE** 13 rue de l'Ancienne-Comedie, 6e.
•0800-0200. M Odéon •Carte 200F, menu 70F.
*Oldest cafe in Paris (founded 1670). Famous rendezvous for intellectuals.*

**LA CLOSERIE DES LILAS** 171 bd du Montparnasse, 6e.
•Open till 0100. M Port-Royal. •Restaurant 300F, Brasserie 150F.
*Two restaurants, terrace and piano bar. Popular with showbiz and literary
people. See* **Montparnasse**.

**BISTRO ROMAIN** 103 bd du Montparnasse, 6e.
•1130-0100. M Montparnasse-Bienvenüe, Vavin. •120F.
*One of a chain of inexpensive bistros with fast, friendly service.*

**TSUKIZI** 2 bis, rue des Ciseaux, 6e.
•1200-1400, 1900-2300 Tues.-Sun. Closed Sun. lunch.
M St-Germain-des-Prés.•150F-200F.
*Pleasant little* sushi *bar, excellent value.*

**BRASSERIE LIPP** 151 bd St-Germain, 6e.
•1200-0200. Closed 23 Dec.-2 Jan. M St-Germain-des-Prés.
•200F-300F.
*Mingle with the journalists, writers and politicians who congregate in this
world-famous restaurant.*

**AUX CHARPENTIERS** 10 rue Mabillon, 6e.
•1200-1500, 1900-2330 Mon.-Sat. Closed 25-31 Dec.
M Mabillon. •100F-150F.
*Traditional French cooking in a very old bistro established in 1856.*

**LA MÉDITERRANÉE** 2 Place de l'Odéon, 6e.
•1200-1500, 1900-2400. M Odéon/RER Luxembourg. •300F.
*Meeting place for writers and artists in the 50s, including Cocteau.*

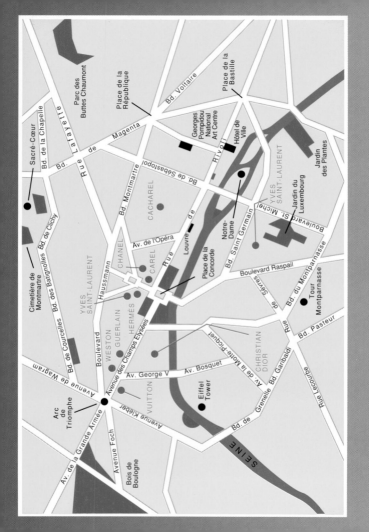

## Luxury

**CHANEL** 31 rue Cambon, 1er.
•1000-1900 Mon.-Sat. M Madeleine.
*World-famous as the birth place of haute couture, also selling ready-to-wear clothing in a magnificent setting.*

**YVES SAINT-LAURENT** 38 rue du Faubourg-St-Honoré, 8e.
•1000-1900. Mon.-Sat. (closed Mon. morning). M Madeleine.
*Beautiful clothes and shoes signed by one of France's top designers.*

**CHRISTIAN DIOR** 30 av Montaigne, 8e.
•1000-1900 Mon.-Sat. (closed Mon. morning). M Franklin-D-Roosevelt.
*A major attraction: superb scarves, jewellery and accessories.*

**CACHAREL** 5 pl des Victoires, 1er.
•1000-1900 Mon.-Sat. (closed Mon. morning). M Sentier.
*World-famous for its classic and tasteful designs.*

**HERMÈS** 24 rue du Faubourg-St-Honoré, 8e.
•1000-1900 Mon.-Sat. (closed Mon. morning). M Madeleine.
*Exceptional quality, status-symbol scarves and saddles.*

**VUITTON** 78 bis, av Marceau, 8e.
•1000-1900 Mon.-Sat. (closed Mon. morning). M Étoile.
*Ultimate designer of bags, luggage and accessories.*

**GUERLAIN** 68 av des Champs-Élysées, 8e.
•1000-1900 Mon.-Sat. M George-V.
*Known worldwide as the Paris perfumer.*

**WESTON** 114 av des Champs-Élysées, 8e.
•1000-1900 Mon.-Sat. (closed Mon. morning). M George-V.
*The most prestigious shoe shop in Paris.*

**CAREL** 22 rue Royale, 8e.
•1000-1900 Mon.-Sat. (closed Mon. morning). M Madeleine.
*The best place to go for elegant, highly-fashionable footwear.*

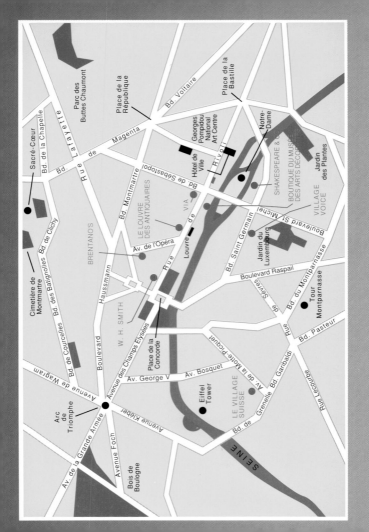

## Miscellaneous

**LE LOUVRE DES ANTIQUAIRES** 2 pl du Palais, 1er.
• 1100-1900 Mon.-Sat. M Palais-Royal.
*World famous art market comprising 250 antique shops.*

**LE VILLAGE SUISSE** 78 av de Suffren, 7e,
55 av de La Motte-Picquet, 15e.
• 1100-1900 Tues., Wed. M La Motte-Picquet-Grenelle.
*Originally built for the 1900 exhibition. Contains a selection of antique dealers.*

**VIA** 2 pl Ste-Opportune, 1er.
• 0930-1900 Mon.-Sat. RER Châtelet-les-Halles.
*Avant-garde designs collected together from all over Europe.*

## BOUTIQUE DU MUSÉE DES ARTS DÉCORATIFS
107 rue de Rivoli, 1er
• 1200-1800 Mon., Wed.-Sat. M Palais-Royal, Tuileries.
*Type of design centre: stationery, cutlery, industrial objects, materials, etc.*

**W. H. SMITH** 248 rue de Rivoli, 1er.
• 0900-1830 Mon.-Sat. M Concorde.
*British books, magazines and newspapers: tea-room upstairs.*

**BRENTANO'S** 37 av de l'Opéra, 2e.
• 1000-1900 Mon.-Sat. M Opéra.
*Bilingual bookstore with an American atmosphere.*

**SHAKESPEARE & CO** 37 rue de la Bûcherie, 5e.
• 1200-2400. M Maubert-Mutualité.
*Friendly English-language bookshop, containing a vast and varied selection of second-hand titles.*

**VILLAGE VOICE** 6 rue Princesse, 6e.
• 1100-2000 Tues.-Sat., 1400-2000 Mon. M Mabillon.
*English-language bookshop named after (but not associated with) the famous American newspaper.*

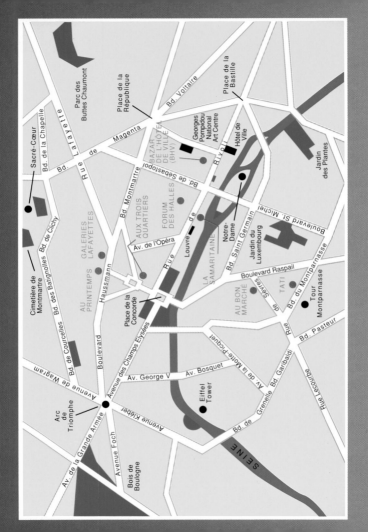

## Dept Stores

**AU PRINTEMPS** 64 bd Hausmann, 9e.
•0935-1830 Mon.-Sat. M Chausée-d'Antin, Havre-Caumartin.
*Worth visiting for women's and men's fashions, accessories and perfumes.*

**GALERIES LAFAYETTES** 40 bd Hausmann, 9e.
•0930-1830 Mon.-Sat. M Chausee d'Antin, Havre-Caumartin.
*The city's major department store, popular with tourists and locals alike.*

**LA SAMARITAINE** 19 rue de la Monnaie, 1er.
•0930-1900 Mon., Wed., Thurs., Sat., 0930-2030 Tues., Fri.
M Pont-Neuf.
*An amazing building housing a famous department store: most definitely a consumers' paradise.*

**AU BON MARCHÉ** 38 rue de Sèvres, 7e.
•0930-1830 Mon.-Sat. M Sèvres-Babylone.
*Established in 1852, the oldest department store in Paris. Fascinating antique shop.*

**AUX TROIS QUARTIERS** 17 bd de la Madeleine, 1er.
•0930-1830 Mon.-Sat. M Madeleine.
*Traditional French department store: interesting range of goods.*

**BAZAR DE L'HÔTEL DE VILLE (BHV)** 52-64 rue de Rivoli, 4e.
•0900-1830 Mon., Tues., Thurs.-Sat., 0900-2200 Wed.
M Hôtel de Ville.
*Wide range of furniture, household goods and DIY on five floors.*

**TATI** 140 rue de Rennes, 6e.
•0900-1900 Mon.-Sat. M Montparnasse-Bienvenüe.
*Superb bargain clothes, well-stocked and cheap. Often crowded.*

**FORUM DES HALLES** 1-7 rue Pierre-Lescot, 1er.
•1000-1930 Tues.-Sat., 1300-1930 Mon. RER Châtelet-les-Halles.
*Huge shopping complex on three levels containing no less than180 shops, 15 restaurants and 10 cinemas.*

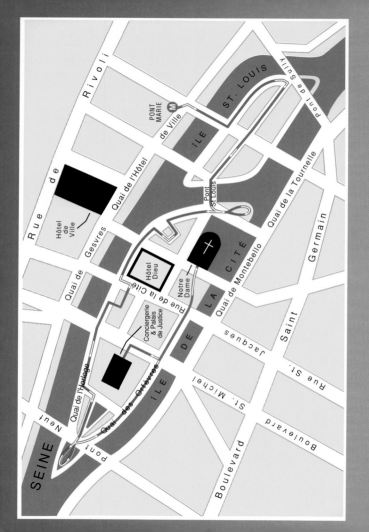

## The Islands

*2 hr.* Start at M Pont Marie.

Cross the bridge and turn left into quai d'Anjou before descending the steps to the quay, where you can enjoy a gentle stroll along the river. Return to the road at Pont Sully and turn right into the long, narrow rue St-Louis-en-l'Île, the island's main street, lined with grand 17thC houses and interesting little shops. At No. 31 is Berthillon with the best ice-cream in Paris. Cross the Pont St Louis onto the Île de la Cité, then left to the square de l'Île de France and visit the deeply moving Mémorial de la Déportation (built to commemorate the 200,000 French citizens who died in Nazi concentration camps).

After leaving the square, turn right into quai aux Fleurs, then left at the rue des Chantres, right at rue Chanoinesse and right again into rue de la Colombe. These small and narrow streets still retain something of the atmosphere of old Paris. Turn left along quai de la Corse, past the Hôtel-Dieu Hospice and left again into place Louis-Lépine. A flower market is held in this square six days a week with a bird market on Sundays (see **MARKETS**).

From here you can see the sombre facade of the Prefecture of Police and, if you continue along the quay to the Tour de l'Horloge, you will come to the first public clock in Paris (1334).

Carry on, taking a left turn into rue Harlay, then right at the lovely place Dauphine (home of the actress Simone Signoret until her death in 1985). At the far end of the place go through the passage, then cross the street and descend the stairs behind the statue of Henri IV. The stair-way takes you into the square du Vert-Galant.

Returning to the Pont Neuf, travel along quai des Orfèvres and turn left when you reach bd du Palais. From here, you can visit the Palais de Justice and also the beautiful church of Sainte Chapelle (see **CHURCHES**, **A-Z**), before retracing your steps to Pont St Michel. Next, turn left along quai Marché-Neuf, cross rue de la Cité and head towards place du Parvis Notre Dame which has superb views of the incomparable Notre Dame Cathedral (see **CHURCHES**, **MUSTS**, **A-Z**). Note the brass star set within the cobbles at the front of the Cathedral. This is 'Point Zero', from where all road distances in France are measured. Round off your walk with a visit to the magnificent Notre Dame itself.

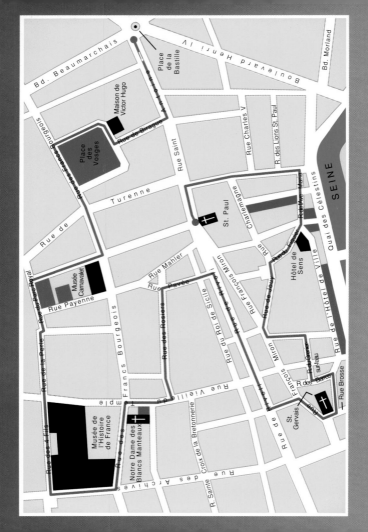

## Le Marais

*2 hr, excluding visits.* Start at M St-Paul-le-Marais.

Head down rue St Antoine towards the Hôtel de Sully (which dates from the early 17thC) at No. 62. Turn left into rue de Birague and into the imposing place des Vosges. To the right, under the arches, is the home of Victor Hugo (see **MUSEUMS 2**). Turn left through the narrow, bustling rue des Francs-Bourgeois, then right at rue de Sévigné. No. 23 houses the Musée Carnavalet (see **MUSEUMS 2**). Turn left along rue du Parc-Royal to place de Thorigny. Continue along rue de la Perle and rue des

Place des Vosges

Quatres-Fils, turning left at rue des Archives with its massive Hôtel de Soubise (home of the National Archives). Continuing along rue des Francs-Bourgeois you pass the little church of Notre Dame des Blancs Manteaux before turning right at rue Vieille-du-Temple, and then left into rue des Rosiers. This is the heart of the Jewish quarter, with most interesting delicatessens, bakers, *etc.* Turn right at rue Pavée, one of the first paved streets in the city. Bear right into the rue de Rivoli and continue on to the place Baudoyer. At the far right side, walk to the St Gervais church (built 15th-17thCs and where François Couperin was organist from 1689-1723) and then into rue de Brosse. Turn left and left again into the rue des Barres and then right into rue du Grenier sur l'Eau. Turn left again and then right into the rue Francois Miron, where you can see at Nos. 11 and 13, two of the oldest houses in Paris, dating from the 14thC. Turn down rue de Jouy, cross rue de Fourcy and turn right into rue du Figuier with the Hôtel de Sens (see **Libraries**). Turn left at rue de l'Ave Maria, pass the rue des Jardins St-Paul and left through the arch into the renovated courtyards of Village St-Paul. At the far end enjoy the lovely rue Charlemagne, before turning right then left at rue St-Paul, and left into rue St-Antoine completing the walk at the 17thC church of St Paul, near M St-Paul-le-Marais.

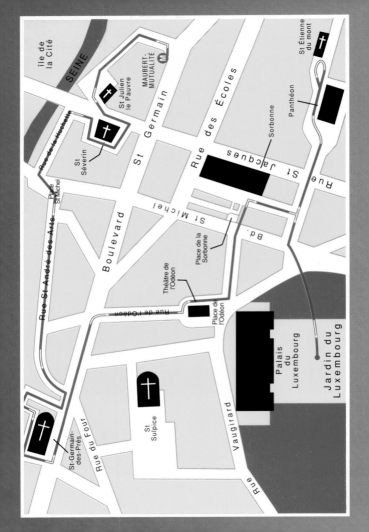

## Latin Quarter

*2 hr, excluding visits.* Begin at M Maubert-Mutualité.

From place Maubert, head along rue Frédéric-Sauton towards the river, then left into rue de la Bûcherie. Cross rue Lagrange into the pleasant square Viviani. Turn left after the church into rue St-Jacques, right at rue de la Parcheminerie, right into rue Boutebrie. Turn right at rue St-Severin, left at the narrow passageway, then left into the rue de la Huchette with its numerous Greek kebab shops. At the end of the street is place St-Michel, centre of the Latin Quarter (see **CITY DISTRICTS, A-Z**). Across the square is the place St-André-des-Arts where you'll find pavement cafés, restaurants, *etc*. Walk along rue St-André-des-Arts, then follow rue de Buci to bd St-Germain, turning right then right again into the passage de la Petite-Boucherie. The quaint, curving rue Cardinale leads left into the charming place de Fustembourg with its white, globe lamp posts and the Musée Delacroix. Turn right at rue de l'Abbaye into place St-Germain-des-Prés.

Sorbonne

The square contains much of interest, from the Church of St-Germain-des-Prés (see **CHURCHES**) to the famous café Les Deux Magots (see **CAFÉS**). Go left along the boulevard to the carrefour de l'Odéon, then right at rue de l'Odéon towards the colonnaded portico of the Théâtre de l'Odéon, left to rue de Vaugirard and across the bd St-Michel to the lovely place de la Sorbonne lined with cafés and full of students.

From the square turn right along the front of the Sorbonne, then left at rue Soufflot where you have a superb view of the Panthéon (see **A-Z**). Go up the hill and the visitors' entrance is at the far side. Returning down rue Soufflot, cross the bd St-Michel and complete your walk with a stroll round the beautiful Luxembourg Gardens (see **MUSTS, PARKS, A-Z**).

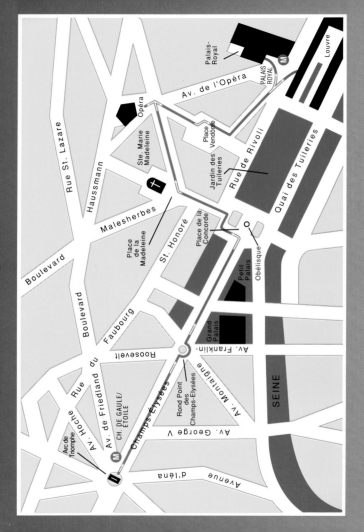

## Champs-Élysées

*2 hr, excluding visits.* Begin at RER Charles-De-Gaulle.

Begin by climbing the 284 steps of the Arc de Triomphe (see **A-Z**) and sampling the magnificent views. Then head down the Champs-Élysées (see **MUSTS**, **A-Z**), past the Tourist Information Office on the left, the famous Lido Cabaret on the right, and the café-restaurant, Le Fouquet's (see **CAFÉS**) at the junction of av George-V. Carry on to the Rond-Point des Champs-Élysées where the character of the avenue changes and it becomes more open and park-like. Stop to enjoy the view along av Winston-Churchill from pl Clemenceau. On the other side of the place is the site of the Marché aux Timbres, held on Thursdays and weekends (see **MARKETS**). Continue to the place de la Concorde (see **A-Z**) and admire the Marly Horses, before looking west, back to the Arc de Triomphe; east to the Tuileries Gardens (see **PARKS**) and Louvre (see **ART GALLERIES**, **MUSEUMS 1**, **MUSTS**, **A-Z**); south to the columns of the Palais-Bourbon; then north to the matching columns of La Madeleine (see **CHURCHES**) where the American embassy occupies a prime location. Passing between the Hôtel Crillon and the Hôtel de la Marine, up the rue Royale you will see the famous Maxim's restaurant and the rue du Faubourg-St-Honoré (see **Fashion**) on your left. Visit La Madeleine before turning right along bd de la Madeleine and bd des Capucines to place de l'Opéra and the splendid facade of the Opéra itself (see **MUSIC VENUES**, **A-Z**). Taking a right turn down rue de la Paix, be sure to appreciate the windows full of luxury goods, then on to place Vendôme (see **A-Z**) and the Ritz. At the far side of the square, exit right along rue St-Honoré, finishing at place du Palais-Royal where you can either visit the Jardin du Palais-Royal or the Louvre.

L'Opéra

## Montmartre

*1:40 hr.* Begin at M Anvers.

Walk up rue de Steinkerque to the Funiculaire de Montmartre (funicular railway) and take a ride up the hill, or climb the steps to the square Willette. A few more steps lead to the place du Parvis and the Sacré-Coeur (see **CHURCHES**, **A-Z**), with its distinctive white domes. From here there is a superb view over the city, as well as the elegant interiors of the basilica to admire. A particular attraction is the enormous mosaic portraying Christ and His followers.

Turn right into rue du Cardinal-Guibert, then left at rue du Chevalier-de-la-Barre and left again at rue du Mont-Cenis. From here admire the church of St-Pierre-de-Montmartre which had its origins in medieval times. Soak up the atmosphere of Montmartre by strolling around the place du Tertre, admiring the skills of the artists.

Exit by rue du Calvaire and turn right into place du Calvaire - a quiet, country-like area with the Historial waxworks museum at 11 rue Poulbot. The exhibits reflect the history of the area. From here travel right along rue Poulbot, then down rue des Saules and right along rue Cortot to the Montmartre Museum, also worth a look. The building itself was home to many artists over the years.

At the end of rue Cortot turn left into rue du Mont-Cenis and down the steps to rue St-Vincent. Go left through the Montmartre vineyard, which is the last one in Paris. A lively wine festival is held here every year at the beginning of October (see **Events**). Rejoin rue des Saules and turn left uphill and right again along rue de l'Abreuvoir to the allée des Brouillards. At the far end, turn left down the steps and up into the square Suzanne-Buisson.

On leaving the square at the far end, you turn right into rue Girardon, across avenue Junot and right into rue Lepic at Moulin Radet (Van Gogh lived at No. 54). Continue along rue Lepic, then turn right at rue Joseph-de-Maistre to the crossroads, taking the left to rue Caulaincourt and down the steps at the end of the bridge to the Cimetière de Montmartre.

Return along rue Joseph-de-Maistre and rue des Abbesses, then left up rue Ravignan to place Émile-Goudeau, right down passage des Abbesses to the lovely place des Abbesses and its church of St-Jean-l'Évangéliste, completing your walk at M Abbesses.

**Accidents and Breakdowns:** If an accident occurs and no-one has been injured, you should fill in the form *Constat à l'Aimable* with full details. Make sure it is signed by both parties and sent to the appropriate insurance companies. You might check with your own insurance company to see if they have similar forms for use in France. If somebody has been injured, contact the police (see **Emergencies**).
Breakdowns: AA and RAC members are entitled to use the services of the Automobile Club de France (6 pl de la Concorde, 8e) and the Touring Club de France (65 av de la Grande Armée, 16e). The RAC has a Paris office at 8 pl Vendôme, 1er. You can obtain a list of emergency breakdown points from the clubs in Britain. See **Driving**.

**Accommodation:** Although there are hundreds of hotels in Paris, it is always advisable to book in advance, especially during peak periods, which include Easter, June, September and October. The French Government Tourist Offices (see **Tourist Information**) issue a list of the most heavily booked periods, based on dates of trade fairs, *etc.*
*Hotels:* There are five categories of hotel: *(basic), **(comfortable), ***(very comfortable), ****(high class), *****(luxury). A double room costs anything between 150F-1000F a night. The more expensive hotels are situated in the 1er, 2e, 8e, 16e and 17e *arrondissements* (see **A-Z**);

Arc de Triomphe

the cheaper, more basic hotels are on the Left Bank (see **CITY DISTRICTS**, **MUSTS**, **WALK 3**, **A-Z**). A complete list of hotels, *Annulaire des Hôtels et Pensions*, is available from French Tourist Offices.

You will find booking facilities at the main Tourist Office, 127 av des Champs-Élysées, 8e, and at Gare d'Austerlitz, Gare du Nord, Gare de l'Est, and Gare de Lyon. They offer help with last-minute difficulties, but don't necessarily guarantee the best deal. For young people, the *Accueil des Jeunes en France* will assist in finding low-cost accommodation: 119 rue St-Martin, 4e; 139 bd-St-Michel, 5e. Open 0930-1900 Mon.-Sat. Other branches at Gare du Nord and 16 rue du Pont-Loius-Phillipe, 4e, are closed from November to February.

For Bed & Breakfast accommodation, contact Paris Rêveries, 179 bd Voltaire, 11e. A double room will cost about 180F.

Student halls of residence are available from July to September through *Accueil des Jeunes en France*. See **Youth Hostels**.

**Airports:** Paris has two international airports: Charles de Gaulle (CDG), at Roissy, 27 km north east of the city; and Orly South and West, 14 km to the south. CDG has two terminals, with a free shuttle bus between. Both airports have all the usual facilities which include banks, currency exchange, medical services, car rental, SNCF desk (see **Railways**), restaurants and bars.

From Charles de Gaulle: Air France coaches run to Porte Maillot every 15 min between 0545-2300 (journey takes 45 min). For Roissy-Rail, take the shuttle to the railway station, and then the RER (see **Railways**) to Gare du Nord (every 15 min, 0500-2315, journey 35 min). For RATP buses, service 350 runs from the airport terminals to Gare de l'Est and Gare du Nord, service 351 goes to pl de la Nation (takes 45-60 min).

From Orly: Air France coaches run to Gare des Invalides or take the Orly bus to M/RER Denfert-Rochereau, both leave every 15 min, 0600-2300 (takes 35 min). Alternatively take the Orly Rail, RER line C, trains go to Gare d'Austerlitz, every 15 min 0530-2330.

**Arc de Triomphe:** A magnificent triumphal arch, commissioned by Napoleon (see **A-Z**) in 1806 as a tribute to his army. Eventually completed in 1836 during the reign of Louis-Philippe, it stands 50 m high and 45 m wide and is decorated with sculptured reliefs depicting military events. The Unknown Soldier lies under the Arc and the Eternal Flame burns in front. From the top you can enjoy the views down the Champs-Élysées (see **WALK 4**, **A-Z**) to the pl de la Concorde (see **WALK 4**, **A-Z**) and the Louvre (see **ART GALLERIES**, **MUSEUMS 1**, **MUSTS**, **A-Z**). 1000-1800; 22F. Place Charles-de-Gaulle-Étoile, 8e. M Étoile. See **WALK 4**.

**Arrondissements:** The area of Paris bounded by the ring road (*boulevard périphérique*) is divided into 20 administrative districts called *arrondissements*. Each one is very individual with its own town hall and a distinct atmosphere. Starting at the Louvre (see **ART GALLERIES**, **MUSEUMS 1**, **MUSTS**, **A-Z**) they radiate in a clockwise direction, and are referred to as 1st, 2nd, 3rd, *etc*. In French these are 1er (*premier*), 2e (*deuxième*), 3e (*troisième*), *etc*, and are included in city addresses.

**Bastille, La:** Built in the 14thC, it was initially used as a fortress, then from the 17thC onwards it became a state prison housing political prisoners, many of whom were kept without trial. Inmates included Voltaire, the Marquis de Sade, and the mysterious 'Man in the Iron Mask'. On 14 July, 1789, a revolutionary mob stormed the prison, lynching the governor and freeing the seven prisoners. This event marked the start of the French Revolution, and its anniversary is celebrated each year on Bastille Day (see **Quatorze Juillet**).

**Bastille, Place de la:** A major traffic intersection standing on the site of the Bastille (see **A-Z**). Paving stones mark the position of the building. It is dominated by the July Column and is also the site of the city's new Opera House which opened on 14 July, 1989.

**Bateaux-Mouches:** These glass-roofed boats sail up and down the Seine (see **A-Z**) providing sightseeing tours. During the evening there are floodlit trips, and you can also dine on board.
Boats depart from Ponte de l'Alma on the right bank (M Alma Marceau) every 30 min 1000-1200, 1400-1800 daily; duration 75 min; cost 20F.
Floodlit trips depart every 30 min 2030-2200; cost 25F.
Meals: lunch on board, dep. 1300 Tues. -Sun.; duration 1hr 45 min;

cost 250F (300F Sun.) incl. wine and service. Dinner (reservations and smart dress required), dep. 2030 Tues.-Sun.; duration 2hr 30 min; cost 450F incl. wine and service. Tel: 42.25.96.10.
Other companies offer similar trips: *Pariscope* (see **Newspapers**, **What's On**) has details, under *'Promenades'*. See **MUSTS**.

**Bibliothèque Nationale:** The National Library, where every book published in France since 1537 is kept - today it holds over 7,000,000 volumes. As well as books, the Library houses the Medailles Collection (coins, medals, medallions and other works of art), and also the State Room with the famous statue of the writer Voltaire, whose heart is buried within the pedestal. 2e. See **Libraries**.

**Bicycle and Scooter Hire:** The traffic in Paris can be extremely dangerous, making the use of either unadvisable. If you do decide to hire however, you have to produce a passport or identity card, and proof of a Paris address. A crash helmet is compulsory for mopeds, and as these are not provided you must find one yourself. The minimum age for hiring a moped is 18. A refundable deposit is required.
For bicycle hire: *Paris-Vélo*, 2 rue du Fer-à-Moulin, 5e.
Tel: 43.37.59.22. 60-140F per day. 1000-1200, 1400-1900 Mon.-Sat.

**Bois de Boulogne:** *Le Bois*, as it is known locally, is situated to the west of the 16e *arrondissement* (see **A-Z**) and occupies 800 hectares of wooded parkland. As well as offering attractive walks and picnic spots, there are: Jardins d'Acclimation (see **CHILDREN**), Musée National des Arts et Traditions Populaires (see **MUSEUMS 2**), Bagatelle gardens, a riding school, bicycle hire, boating on the ornamental lake, the racecourses of Auteuil and Longchamp (see **Sports**) and restaurants. It is not advisable to wander into the *Bois* at night. M Porte Maillot, Porte d'Auteuil, Porte Dauphine.

**Bois de Vincennes:** This is the second major park in Paris, sitting on the right bank of the Seine (see **A-Z**), to the south east of the city. Here you will find the Château de Vincennes, Floral Gardens with roses and azaleas on display, a horticultural school, boating lakes, a racecourse, an arboretum, boules pitches, a Buddhist centre with Tibetan temple, the Cartoucherie de Vincennes (once an ammunition factory, now a theatre complex), and the Parc Zoologique, the city's zoo (see **CHILDREN**). M Porte Dorée, Château de Vincennes.

## Budget:

| | |
|---|---|
| *Inexpensive:* | One night in a youth hostel: 53F |
| | Meal in a fixed-price menu restaurant: 70F |
| | Meal in a fast-food restaurant: 35F |
| | Visit to two museums: 50F |
| | Movie: 35F |
| | Any transport (*carte orange*): 43F per week |
| *Moderate:* | One night in a two star hotel: 300F |
| | Two average meals fixed-price menu: 200F |
| | Travel (*billet de tourisme*): 150F per week |
| | Visit to two museums: 50F |
| | Movie: 35F |
| *Expensive:* | One night in a four star hotel: 1,000F |
| | Two meals in a good restaurant: 600F |
| | Travel by taxi (4 av trips): 200F |
| | Visit to two museums: 50F |
| | Cabaret (without dinner): 350F |

**Buses:** The city bus service is run by RATP, as is the *Métro* (see **A-Z**), and it is both efficient and easy to use. Bus stops are painted red and yellow, with route numbers clearly marked, and the bus shelters have maps showing the routes, times and fares - each bus has its route number displayed on the front, back and side. All buses operate from 0700-2030, and some run until midnight. You can obtain route maps free from any *Métro* station. There is a night bus service which runs hourly from pl du Châtelet. Reduced services operate on Sundays.

Tickets on the buses are the same as on the *Métro*. Punch your ticket (*compostez votre billet*) in the machine beside the driver, or if you have a *carte orange* or *billet de tourisme*, just show it to him. The cost is one or two tickets depending on the length of your journey. The RATP also run excursions to locations outside the city. For a brochure, contact RATP offices or railway stations. See **Transport**.

**Cameras and Photography:** Photography is very popular with the Parisians, and you will find good quality film and equipment readily available. A fast processing service is offered by the FNAC shop, *niveau* (level)-3, Forum des Halles, 1er. Check with staff before using a camera in museums or art galleries, as there are usually restrictions. In the Louvre, for example, hand-held cameras are admitted free, but you will have to pay if you wish to use a tripod, and flashes are prohibited.

**Camping and Caravanning:** There is only one site in the city itself: Camping Île de France, allée du Bord-de-l'Eau, 16e, in the Bois de Boulogne (see **A-Z**). M Porte Maillot, tel: 45.06.14.98. It has 500 places, but is usually full in summer. For information on sites around Paris, contact: Camping Club de France, 218 bd St-Germain, 7e; or Fédération Française de Camping et Caravaning, 78 rue de Rivoli, 4e.

**Car Hire:** To hire a car you must produce a passport and a current driving licence which has been valid for at least one year. A cash deposit is necessary, unless paying by credit card, and also proof of a Paris address. The minimum age is 21-25, depending on the company. Be sure to check the basis of charge, *ie a* daily rate plus so much per kilometre, or unlimited mileage. Third party insurance is compulsory.

Sacré-Coeur

For full details contact the Tourist Office (see **Tourist Information**).
Cat A: 230F per day & 2,72F per km; 2320F per week, with unlimited
mileage. VW Golf, or similar, 2225F for five days, unlimited mileage.
*Avis* - 5 rue Bixio, 7e. Tel: 45.50.32.31.
*Europcar* - 145 av Malakoff, 16e. Tel: 45.00.08.06 (many offices).

**Champs-Élysées:** This 2 km-long avenue stretches between pl de la
Concorde (see **A-Z**) and the Étoile (see **A-Z**) and was once thought to
be the most beautiful avenue in the world. Dating from the 17thC, it
was planted with trees to extend the view from the Tuileries (see **PARKS**).
In 1709 the area was named the Champs-Élysées (Elysian Fields), and
by 1828 the avenue had gas-lighting, pavements and aristocratic resi-
dences, making it a very fashionable promenade.
Today the area is somewhat commercialized, and the section between
Rond Point and Étoile is lined with shops, banks, cinemas, fast-food
outlets, car showrooms and airline offices. Even so, the views from
Étoile or pl de la Concorde are quite magnificent, and the pavement
cafés provide a most interesting spot from which to sit and watch the
world go by. 8e. M/RER Étoile-Charles-de-Gaulle, George-V, Franklin-
D-Roosevelt, Clemenceau, Concorde. See **WALK 4**.

**Chantilly:** The famous *château* on the lakeside here is in two parts:
the Grand Château, and the Petit Château d'Enghien. You can also visit
the Musée Condé, which has an interesting collection of 15th-17thC
paintings, sculptures, drawings, ceramics and furniture, and the Cabinet
de Livres, which houses over 12,500 rare books and manuscripts.
Amongst them is the Duc de Berri's *Book of Hours* - one of the finest
illuminated manuscripts in the world. See **EXCURSIONS 1**.

**Chartres:** The town of Chartres, 90 km south of Paris, is best known
for its Gothic cathedral, one of the world's finest. It has magnificent
stained glass windows dating from the 12th and 13thCs, and beautifully
carved portals, nave and choir. See **EXCURSION 4**.

**Chemists:** There are plenty of chemists (easily identified by their
green cross signs) throughout the city. Most open 1400-1930 Mon.,

0900-1930 Tues.-Sat. For addresses of those which open late and on Sundays, see the notice displayed on each chemist's door.
Two chemists which open 24 hrs: *Pharmacie Les Champs*, 84 av des Champs-Élysées, 8e; and 61 rue de Ponthieu, 8e - both at M Franklin-D-Roosevelt. For English speaking staff: *Pharmacie Anglaise,* 62 av des Champs-Élysées, 8e (closed Sun.). M Franklin-D-Roosevelt.

**Children:** Children are usually made welcome by Parisians. You can quite happily take them to hotels, restaurants, cafés and museums, and there are plenty of activities for them (see **CHILDREN**). For information consult *Pariscope* (see **Newspapers**, **What's On**), or contact: Loisirs-Jeunes, 36 rue de Ponthieu, 8e; Paris Junior, 26 rue Delambre, 14e. Babysitters (*gardes d'enfants*): ABABA, La Maman en Plus!, tel: 43.22.22.11, 0800-2200 daily (English speakers available); Allo Maman Poule, tel: 47.47.78.78, 24 hrs a day. Prices are about 20F per hour plus agency fee, and taxis.

**Cigarettes and Tobacco:** Licensed tobacconists (*tabacs*), displaying red diamond-shaped signs, sell cigarettes and pipe tobacco. You can also buy tobacco goods at *le drugstore* and certain restaurants and bars, but not from automatic vending machines. French brands such as *Gauloises* cost around 5,40F for 20, while foreign brands are slightly more expensive, *eg* 10F for 20 Marlboro.

**Climate:** The seasons are similar to other northern European cities: winters are relatively mild (mean temp. in Nov.-Feb. is 5° C) and dry, but cold spells can send the temperature below zero. Springtime is fairly cool and dry. In summer the mean temperature is 18° C, but rainfall is greatest during the summer and autumn months so come prepared.

**Compiègne:** This extremely large 18thC palace was initially built during the reign of Louis XV and later restored by Napoleon (see **A-Z**). Louis XVI entertained Marie-Antoinette here, and likewise Napoleon his second wife, Empress Marie-Louise. There are ten apartments restored to their former glory and many of the tapestries and pieces of furniture were brought by Napoleon himself. The Palace also houses the Musée National de la Voiture et du Tourisme (Transport Museum) where you can see coaches, carriages, early bicycles and automobiles. 82 km north east of Paris. SNCF Gare du Nord to Compiègne. By Car - A11. 1000-1200, 1330-1700 Wed.-Mon. 7F (3,50F Sun.).

**Conciergerie, La:** This is one of the most famous prisons in France, and part of the old royal palace. Many leading figures of the Revolution, including Marie-Antoinette and Robespierre, were kept here before being led to the guillotine. Today you can visit the huge, vaulted Gothic room of the Salles des Gens d'Armes, the Salles des Gardes, and the kitchen with its enormous fireplace - all dating from the 14thC. 1 quai de l'Horloge, 1er. M Cité. 1000-1800 (1700 winter). 30F (includes entry to Sainte Chapelle, see CHURCHES, A-Z). See WALK 1.

**Concorde, Place de la:** An impressive square with views to La Madeleine (see CHURCHES, WALK 4), the Palais-Bourbon, the Louvre (see ART GALLERIES, MUSEUMS 1, MUSTS, A-Z) and Arc de Triomphe (see A-Z). When laid out in 1755-75, it displayed a statue of Louis XV, then one of La Liberté (during the Revolution), and today it boasts the Obelisk of Luxor. Louis XVI, Marie-Antoinette, Robespierre and Danton were all victims of the guillotine which once stood here. 8e. M Concorde.

Place de la Concorde

**Consulates:**

*Great Britain*: Embassy - 35, rue du Faubourg-St-Honoré, 8e. Tel: 42.66.91.42; Consulate - 16, rue d'Anjou, 8e. Tel: 42.96.87.19.
*USA*: 2, av Gabriel, 8e. Tel: 42.96.12.02.
*Canada*: 35, av Montaigne, 8e. Tel: 47.23.01.01.
*Australia*: 4, rue Jean-Rey. 15e. Tel: 40.59.33.00.
*New Zealand*: 7, rue Léonard-de-Vinci, 16e. Tel: 45.00.24.11.

**Conversion Charts:**

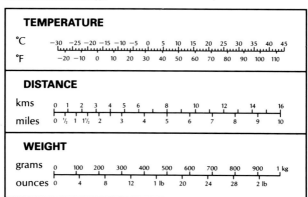

**TEMPERATURE**

°C   −30 −25 −20 −15 −10 −5 0 5 10 15 20 25 30 35 40 45
°F   −20 −10 0 10 20 30 40 50 60 70 80 90 100 110

**DISTANCE**

kms   0 1 2 3 4 5 6 8 10 12 14 16
miles   0 ½ 1 1½ 2 3 4 5 6 7 8 9 10

**WEIGHT**

grams   0 100 200 300 400 500 600 700 800 900 1 kg
ounces   0 4 8 12 1 lb 20 24 28 2 lb

**Crime and Theft:** Special care should always be taken of handbags and wallets, *etc*, as pickpockets are rife on the *Métro*, buses and indeed in any crowded location. Never leave your car unlocked, and be sure to remove or hide any valuables. If you do have anything stolen, report the theft immediately to the nearest police station (*commissariat de police*), and obtain an *attestation de vol* document so that you can claim insurance. You must inform your embassy at once if your passport is stolen (see **Consulates**). In emergencies, dial 17: you will be put through to the local police station. See **Emergencies**, **Police**.

**CUR**    **A-Z**

**Currency:** The French unit of currency is the *franc* which is divided into 100 *centimes*. Bank notes are issued for 500F, 200F, 100F, 50F and 20F. Coins are 10F (two types, the older version is bronze-coloured, the newer ones are smaller with a brass rim and silver centre), 5F, 2F, 1F, 50c (all silver), 20c, 10c, and 5c (all brass). See **Money**.

**Customs:**

| Duty Paid Into: | Cigarettes | *or* Cigars | *or* Tobacco | Spirits | Wine |
|---|---|---|---|---|---|
| E.E.C. | 300 | 75 | 400 g | 1.5 *l* | 5 *l* |
| U.K. | 300 | 75 | 400 g | 1.5 *l* | 5 *l* |

**De Gaulle, Charles (1890-1970):** Soldier and statesman. As leader of the Free French with his headquarters in England during the Second World War, he was the symbol of resistance to German occupation and the Vichy régime. After the Liberation in 1944, he formed a provisional government, but soon retired from politics, critical of France's weak parliamentary system. In 1958, with France on the verge of civil war over Algerian demands for independence, he became the first president of the Fifth Republic. Unable to contain the student revolt of 1968, he resigned after losing a referendum in 1969.

**Dentists:** See Emergencies, Health.

**Disabled Travellers:** For information about accommodation, transport, facilities and aids for the disabled, see the booklet *Touristes Quand Même* supplied by the Tourist Office. See **Tourist Information**.

**Doctors:** See Emergencies, Health.

**Dôme des Invalides:** Also known as Église du Dôme. A domed church, built in 1675-1706, which houses the Tomb of Napoleon (see **A-Z**) - a sarcophagus of red porphyry upon a green Vosges granite pedestal. The dome has a leaded roof and is decorated with gilded trophies and garlands. Av de Tourville, 7e. M Varenne. See **CHURCHES**.

**Drinks:** In France there are no licensing laws, so you can buy alcohol in bars and cafés at any time. House wines are sold by the litre (*une carafe*), half-litre (*un demi-litre*) or quarter litre (*un quart*); a jug (*un pichet*) can hold either a quarter or half-litre.
Beer is usually lager, although you will find a wider selection if you go to a 'pub'. It is quite alright to ask for plain water (*une carafe d'eau*) with a meal, and this comes free.
Coffee: ask for '*un café*' if you wish a small, strong, black espresso; '*un café au lait*' for coffee with milk; and '*un grand crème*' for a large white coffee, the kind usually served at breakfast with croissants.
Tea is growing in popularity, with the best being available at the special '*salons de thé*', otherwise it tends to be pretty awful!
Hot chocolate is simply, '*un chocolat*'.
In cafés, it is less expensive to stand at the bar (*au comptoir*) than to sit down with your coffee and croissants, *etc*. There is also sometimes a difference in price between inside and outside the café, *ie* at a table on the pavement.

**Driving:** Driving in Paris can be a hair-raising experience, and is not recommended. If you intend to travel to Paris by car, you will need a valid national or international driving licence plus insurance documents (a Green Card is no longer necessary for EC members but the AA recommend that you have one anyway), nationality sticker, yellow filters for headlamps, and a red warning triangle. You should, whenever possible, use the ring-road (*boulevard périphérique*) rather than attempt to drive across the city.
The French drive on the right hand side of the road, and at T-junctions, intersections and roundabouts, the traffic from the right has right-of-way; seat-belts are now compulsory for passengers in the front and recommended for those in the back.

Speed-limits: built-up areas 60 kph; Paris ring-road 80 kph; main roads 90/110 kph; motorways (*autoroutes*) 130 kph.

Petrol (*l'essence*): there are plenty of petrol stations around the city, though most are not self-service.

Parking: parking in the city tends to be very restricted, so try the underground car-parks in the city centre and at all the major *portes* on the ring-road (and then take the *Métro* into the centre). Parking meters operate from 0900-1900, and traffic-wardens and police can impose hefty fines or tow away vehicles parked illegally. If your car is impounded, you will have to phone the town hall (*mairie*) in that *arrondissement* to reclaim it. See **Accidents and Breakdowns**.

**Drugs:** In France it is illegal to use or possess any form of narcotics, and anyone caught trying to smuggle drugs into the country faces almost certain imprisonment.

**Eating Out:** This is one of the most enjoyable facets of Parisian life, and need not cost you a fortune either. By law, all restaurants must display their prices outside and have at least one fixed-price menu (*menu fixe* or *formule*) as well as the *à la carte*. These fixed price menus can cost as little as 50F, whereas the *à la carte* is always slightly more expensive. Paris caters for all tastes and budgets, ranging from international and nouvelle cuisine, to traditional French provincial cooking. Contact the Tourist Office for a useful free booklet: *Guide des Restaurants de Paris*.

Restaurants traditionally open 1200-1400, 1900-2200; alternatively you can grab a quick meal in a *brasserie* at almost any time. *Bistros* are similar to *brasseries* but usually cheaper, with a set meal of the day, basic food and quick service.

Cafés serve a variety of drinks all day, as well as snacks such as croissants and *croque-monsieur* (a type of cheese and ham toasted sandwich). Remember - it will cost less to stand at the bar or to eat inside than to sit at a table outside. The *salons de thé* specialize in rather expensive pots of tea with cakes and rich pastries.

If you wish a late night snack, try a '*drugstore*' which provides a similar service to that of the *brasserie*, but is open till 0200.

The best areas for eating out are: the Left Bank (especially St-Germain-des-Prés, bd St-Michel, Latin Quarter and rue Mouffetard), Les Halles, the area around l'Opéra, and the Champs-Élysées. See **RESTAURANTS**.

**Eiffel Tower:** Internationally recognized as the symbol of France, the tower was designed by Gustave Eiffel to mark the centenary of the French Revolution. Opened in May 1889, standing 312 m high, it was the tallest building of its day. There are three platforms, all offering exceptional views, those from the top being positively breathtaking. On a clear day you can see landmarks well outside the suburbs of the city. Champ-de-Mars, 7e. M Trocadéro, Bir-Hakeim. 1000-2300 daily (top level closed mid-Nov.-mid-Mar.). Lift to 3rd level (top), 44F; 2nd level, 28F; 1st level, 12F. By stairs to 1st and 2nd levels, 7F. See **MUSTS**.

**Electricity:** The voltage in Paris is 220V, which is fine for most UK appliances, but plugs and sockets vary greatly and are completely different from those in Britain, so an adaptor is essential (available from most electrical shops).

**Emergencies:**
Police - 17.
Fire Brigade - 18 (call them also if someone is in trouble in the river).
SAMU (24-hr ambulance) - 45.67.50.50.
24-hr emergency doctor (*SOS Médecins*) - 43.37.77.77.
24-hr emergency dentist (*SOS Dentistes*) - 43.37.51.00.
Emergency treatment for poisoning - 42.05.63.29.
Serious burns - 43.46.13.90 (children) - 42.34.17.58 (adults).
Rape Crisis Hotline (English speakers ask for Anne) - 05.05.95.95.
SOS HELP English Crisis Hotline - 47.23.80.80, 1500-2300 daily.
See **Accidents and Breakdowns**, **Health**, **Police**.

**Étoile:** Officially pl Charles-de-Gaulle, this junction is known as l'Étoile (the star) because of the 12 avenues which radiate from it. There are superb views from the top of the Arc de Triomphe (see **A-Z**) at its centre. 8e/16e/17e. M/RER Étoile, Charles-de-Gaulle. See **WALK 4**.

**Events:** The Tourist Office (see **Tourist Information**) issues a list of all city events, and a monthly leaflet on the major ones (*Paris Sélection*).
*January*: Winter sales in the shops; International Boat Show at CNIT, La Défense (2nd or 3rd week).
*March*: Agricultural Show, Parc des Expositions, Porte de Versailles.
*April*: Opening of Foire de Paris (Paris Fair) at Parc des Expositions, Porte de Versailles (late April/early May).
*May*: Labour Day (1st); celebration of Allied Victory 1945 (8th); Paris Air Show at Le Bourget (late May/early June); Soirées de St-Aignan, at Hôtel St Aignan, 18-19thC European music.
*June*: Flower Show in Floral Gardens, Bois de Vincennes (see **A-Z**); Festival du Marais, theatre, dance, mime, music (Marais district, mid-June/mid-July); Summer Solstice (21st) parades (incl. Gay Pride March), street entertainment, *etc*; Festival International de Film Fantastique et de Science-Fiction, at Grand Rex cinema, 1 bd Poissonière, 2e.
*July*: Bastille Day (see **Quatorze Juillet**), military parades in the Champs-Élysées, fireworks, concerts; Paris Summer Music Festival (mid-July/mid-Sept.).
*September*: Festival d'Automne, music, drama (Sept.-Dec.).

*October:* Festival International  de Danse de Paris, ballet, Theatre des Champs-Élysées; Festival d'Art Sacré, religious music, church concerts (Oct.-Nov.); Montmartre Wine Festival, rue des Saules/rue St Vincent (1st or 2nd week); International Contemporary Art Exhibition (FIAC), Grand Palais (early Oct./Dec.); Festival de Jazz (late Oct./early Nov.).
*November:* All Saints' Day (1st); Armistice Day (11th), Arc de Triomphe.
*December:* Midnight Mass in principal churches (24th); New Year's Eve, informal celebrations in Champs-Élysées.

**Fashion:** Paris, fashion centre of the world, has many *haute couture* boutiques. They are mainly concentrated in the rue du Faubourg-St-Honoré (*eg* Hermés, St-Laurent-Rive-Gauche, Lanvin), av Montaigne (Nina Ricci, Christian Dior), St-Germain-des-Pres area, pl des Victoires (Cacharel, Kenzo) and increasingly on the Left Bank (see **CITY DISTRICTS, A-Z**). Many shops sell last year's designer clothes at vastly reduced prices (20-50% off) and you will find these around the 6e *arr.* in the rues de Rennes, de Sèvres and St-Placide. See **SHOPPING 1 & 3, WALK 4**.

**Food:** No nation takes more pride in its cuisine than France, and Paris is undoubtedly one of the world's major gastronomic centres. *Haute cuisine* (classic, rich, and extravagant) may be beyond the average tourist's pocket, and *nouvelle cuisine* (fresh, lightly-cooked and imaginatively-presented) might well be regarded with suspicion, but the high standard of cooking in even the humblest of bistros is sure to please. The archetypal breakfast consists of coffee and *croissants*. *Fromages* (cheeses), cold meats, *patisseries* (pastries), and *baguette* sandwiches will provide sustenance during the day. At dinner, every kind of meat, game, poultry, offal, fish and shellfish is carefully prepared in a huge variety of guises. Some of the favourites are: *escargots* (snails); *bisque* (shellfish soup); *pâté de foie gras* (goose liver pâté); *moules marinière* (mussels and shallots in white wine); *coq au vin* (chicken in red wine); *bouillabaisse* (fish and vegetable stew); *bœuf bourguignon* (beef and vegetables in red wine); *canard à l'orange* (duck in orange sauce); *cassoulet* (pork, goose, sausage and haricot bean casserole); *tournedos Rossini* (fillet of beef stuffed with pâté); *blanquette de veaux* (veal in white sauce); *crêpe suzette* (flambéed pancake); *petits fours* (sweetmeats).

**Hairdressers:** There are plenty of hairdressers (*coiffeurs*) to be found all over the city, though it is usually necessary to make an appointment, especially at the well-known ones. The most famous include:
*Carita*: 11 rue du Faubourg-St-Honoré, 8e. Tel: 42.65.79.00.
*Jacques Dessanges*: 37 av Franklin-D-Roosevelt, 8e. Tel: 43.59.31.31.
*Jean-Louis David*: 38 av de Wagram, 8e. Tel: 47.63.68.91.
*Maniatis*: 10 rue Poquelin, 1er. Tel: 42.96.90.95 and 35 rue de Sèvres, 6e. Tel: 45.44.16.39.
A cut at one of the above will cost you from about 300F-500F at the major salons, and from 150F-250F at the other branches. The local hairdressers are cheaper, with a cut costing an average of 100F-150F.

**Health:** Medical treatment through the French social security system is available to all citizens of EC countries. Residents of the UK should obtain a form E111 from the DSS before you leave. Be warned, you will have to pay for any treatment in the first instance, then claim it back afterwards, which can be a time-consuming, complicated affair. Even an ordinary visit to the doctor costs about 85F, so it certainly pays to take out medical insurance beforehand.
Lists of doctors (including those available on Sundays and holidays) can be obtained from hotels, chemists or police stations. See **Emergencies**.

**Hospitals:** *American Hospital* 63 bd Victor-Hugo, Neuilly-sur-Seine. Tel: 47.47.53.00 (English-speaking).
*British Hospital* 48 rue de Villiers, Levallois-Perret. Tel: 47.58.13.12.

**Île de la Cité:** A small island in the Seine (see **A-Z**) at the city centre which was possibly the earliest part of Paris to be inhabited, maybe even earlier than the 3rdC BC. 1er/4e. M Cité. See **WALK 1**.

**Île St Louis:** The second island in the Seine (see **A-Z**), joined to the Île de la Cité (see **A-Z**) as recently as the 17thC, and now an island in its own right. There are still many old houses to see with views over the Left Bank (see **CITY DISTRICTS, MUSTS, WALK 1, A-Z**) and Notre Dame (see **CHURCHES, MUSTS, WALK 3, A-Z**), and its tranquillity makes it an ideal place for a peaceful stroll. 4e. M Pont Marie. See **WALK 1**.

Île de la Cité

**Invalides, Hôtel des:** Home of three military museums: Musée de l'Armée; Musée de l'Ordre de la Libération (covering various facets of the Second World War); and Musée des Plans-Reliefs (maps, models and detailed plans of French fortifications and military strongholds). M Invalides, Latour-Maubourg. See MUSEUMS 3.

**Latin Quarter:** Student centre on the Left Bank (see CITY DISTRICTS, MUSTS, **A-Z**), opposite the Île de la Cité (see **A-Z**), where many of the University of Paris buildings are situated. The students and professors spoke Latin in its early days, hence the name, and you'll find a wide range of cheap restaurants and hotels here. See CITY DISTRICTS, WALK 3.

**Laundries:** Hotels are generally happy to do your laundry, otherwise you will find many self-service coin-operated launderettes around the city (*blanchisserie-self*). Among those in the centre are:
28 rue Beaubourg, 3e; 24 place du Marché-St-Honore, 1er;
1 rue de la Montagne-Ste-Geneviève, 5e.

**Left Bank:** The area immediately south of the River Seine (see **A-Z**) which includes the Latin Quarter (see CITY DISTRICTS, WALK 3, **A-Z**), St-Germain-des-Prés (see CHURCHES, **A-Z**), Montagne-Ste-Geneviève and Montparnasse (see CITY DISTRICTS, **A-Z**). The University of Paris is large-ly situated here, and the area has long been associated with students, intellectuals, artists, *etc* with a very different atmosphere from that of the commercial Right Bank (see **A-Z**). See CITY DISTRICTS, MUSTS.

**Libraries:** *Bibliothèque Nationale* : Certain areas of the library are open to the public, but a reader's card is required to use the books (0900-2000 Mon.-Fri., 0900-1730 Sat.). 58 rue de Richelieu, 2e. M Bourse, Palais-Royal. See **A-Z**.
*BPI (Bibliothèque Publique d'Information)*: Huge library with an exten-sive English-language section (1200-2200 Mon.,Wed.-Fri. ,1000-2000 Sat.,Sun.). Pompidou Centre, place Beaubourg, 4e. M Rambuteau.
*Bibliothèque Mazarine:* A collection of rare books covering French regional history which is housed in a 17thC mansion (1000-1800 Mon.-Fri.). 23 quai Conti, 6e. M Pont-Neuf.

*Bibliothèque Forney* (Hôtel de Sens): Books on fine arts and crafts kept in a medieval bishop's palace (1330-2000 Tues.-Sat.). 1 rue du Figuier, 4e. M St-Paule-Marais. See **WALK 2**.
There are also libraries at the following Cultural Institutes:
British, 9 rue de Constantine, 7e, and American, 10 rue du Général-Camou, 7e. Both offer free access to an extensive selection of books and periodicals relating to Britain and America.

**Lost Property:** If you lose anything you should contact the *Bureau des Objets Trouvés*, 36 rue des Morillons, 15e. Tel: 48.28.32.36. M Convention. 0830-1700 Mon.-Fri. (2000 Tues., Thurs.).
The airports (see **A-Z**) and major railway stations (see **Railways**) also have their own lost property offices.

**Louvre, Le:** Built between the 16th and 19thCs, this is undoubtedly one of the most famous art galleries in the world. The Palais du Louvre began as a royal residence, and after the Revolution opened as a national art gallery and museum in 1793. Today it is undergoing major expansion and reorganization, which includes the resiting of the entrance under the controversial glass pyramid east of the place du Carrousell.The vast collection is in seven sections: three of antiquities (Oriental, Egyptian, Greek and Roman), sculpture, applied art, graphic art, and paintings. There is so much to see, that a number of trips are recommended. Be warned - it is usually crowded! See **ART GALLERIES, MUSEUMS 1, MUSTS.**

**Luxembourg, Jardin du:** Next to the Palais du Luxembourg, these lovely gardens have much to offer, including tennis courts, pony rides, puppet theatres, ponds and fountains. See **MUSTS, PARKS**.

**Malmaison, Château de:** The Empress Josephine, wife of Napoleon (see **A-Z**) lived here from 1799 until her death in 1814. You can visit both the private and official apartments on the guided tours, seeing many original furnishings in the dining, music and billiard rooms. Napoleon's grey raincoat and his black cocked hat are among the exhibits on view in the nearby Musée de Bois-Préau.

Reuil-Malmaison. RER to La Défense, then bus 158A to Malmaison-Château. Château and museum 1000-1200, 1330-1630, Wed.-Mon. Château 20F (10F Sun.), museum 5F (2,50F Sun.).

**Métro:** Parisians have used the *Métro* since the start of the century (19 July, 1900, to be precise), and its 15 lines and 360 stations save much time and are extremely convenient. It is open from 0530-0030 and dotted all over the city you'll see the distinctive Art-Nouveau entrance signs. Maps may be obtained free from all stations and the Tourist Offices (see **Tourist Information**).

Tickets and special passes are available from RATP booths at the entrance to stations, and from the SNCF desk at CDG-Roissy Airport. A Tourist Ticket (*Billet de Tourisme/Paris Sésame*) will give you seven days unlimited travel on the *Métro*, RER and bus (but not RER Roissy Rail), first class only - 150F. The *Carte Orange* (orange card) is very popular with Parisians and combines an ID card with a passport photo. This lets you buy a weekly ticket for unlimited travel on the *Métro* or bus (valid Monday morning to Sunday evening) for 43F, or monthly, about 150F. A *Formule 1* ticket will provide you with unlimited travel up to Zone 3 on the *metro* and bus for one day, and costs 19F.

For short stays, a *carnet* of ten tickets (30F) often works out cheaper, with a flat rate of one per journey (remember to retain it till the end of your journey - an inspector may ask to see it).

**Mona Lisa**: Leonardo da Vinci painted *La Joconde* (as it is known in France) in 1505, and it is probably the best-known painting in the world. It is permanently on view in the Salle des États on the first floor of the Louvre (see **ART GALLERIES**, **MUSEUMS 1**, **MUSTS**, **A-Z**).

**Money:** The two main banks in Paris are the BNP (*Banque National de Paris*) and CL (*Crédit Lyonnais*), which open 0830-1630 Mon.-Fri. Banks which open on Saturday include: Crédit Commercial de France, 115 av des Champs-Élysées, 8e (0830-1945); and BNP, 49 av des Champs-Élysées and 2 pl de l'Opéra (mornings only).

There are exchange facilities at airports and mainline railway stations, plus many *bureaux de change* in the centre of the city. Some banks, but

Montmartre

ontmartre

not all, will also change money and travellers cheques. Exchange rates and commission charges vary from bank to bank so it pays to look around. For late opening exchange: Société Financière de Change Lincoln, 11 rue Lincoln, 8e (1000-2400 daily).

Credit cards are widely accepted with Visa (*Carte Bleu*) being the most common, so look out for the appropriate signs on doors and windows. The American Express office is at 11 rue Scribe, 9e. Tel: 42.66.09.99. M Opéra. 0900-1730 Mon.-Sat.

Traveller's cheques are probably the safest way to carry holiday money, and can be used in a great many locations, though not in some of the cheaper hotels and restaurants. You will find them easy to exchange at any bank or *bureau de change*. See **Currency**.

**Montmartre:** A picturesque area which still manages to retain a vil-lage-like atmosphere. It is dominated by the white domed Sacré-Cœur (see **CHURCHES, A-Z**). In the 19thC many writers and artists frequented Montmartre, *eg* Baudelaire, Berlioz, Toulouse-Lautrec, Van Gogh, Picasso and Modigliani, but nowadays tourists completely dominate the area. If you climb or take the funicular railway to the top of the hill (*butte*), you can enjoy some of the most breathtaking views over Paris. 18e. M Abbesses, Anvers. See **CITY DISTRICTS, MUSTS, WALK 5**.

**Montparnasse:** An area on the Left Bank (see **CITY DISTRICTS, MUSTS, WALK 3, A-Z**) which replaced Montmartre (see **CITY DISTRICTS, MUSTS, WALK 5, A-Z**) as the Bohemian centre of Paris in the late 19th and early 20thCs. Some of the famous who frequented the area included James Joyce, Hilaire Belloc, Scott Fitzgerald, Henry Miller and Ernest Hemingway - who lived here at 113 rue Notre-Dame-des-Champs, and wrote at the Closerie des Lilas Café (see **RESTAURANTS 4**). Europe's tallest building, the 59-storey Tour Maine-Montparnasse, dominates the area and has a shopping complex at its base and a bar and shop on the 56th floor (1000-2200. 31F to 59th floor, 50F to 56th). At the Cimetière du Montparnasse you can find the graves of Guy de Maupassant, Jean-Paul Sartre, Baudelaire, and André Citroën, among others. 6e/14e/15e. M Montparnasse-Bienvenüe, Raspail. See **CITY DISTRICTS, Left Bank.**

**Mouffetard, Rue:** A narrow and lively street which winds downhill from place de la Contrescarpe with little old shops, houses and small restaurants on either side. Do try to visit the daily food market if you get a chance. 5e. M Censier-Daubenton, Monge. See **MARKETS.**

**Moulin Rouge:** Birth place of the Can-Can, this extremely famous nightclub was opened in 1883 and its early days were recorded in the paintings of Toulouse-Lautrec. Today it is still very popular, though mostly with tourists. 82 bd de Clichy, 18e. M Blanche.

**Music:** Paris has music to satisfy all tastes:
*Classical* - at l'Opéra (see **WALK 4**, **A-Z**), and the numerous concert halls (*eg* Salles Pleyel and Cortot, Théâtre des Champs-Élysées, Châtelet, Maison de la Radio). A comprehensive list can be seen in *Pariscope* and *l'Officiel des Spectacles* (see **Newspapers**, **What's On**).
*Contemporary music* - the IRCAM at the Pompidou Centre is the place to go, though more varied and popular styles can be heard at the Olympia, Théâtre de la Ville, Palais des Congrès and Zénith. Tickets are available from box offices and FNAC bookstores (Forum des Halles; av de Wagram; Maine-Montparnasse shopping centre). See **MUSIC VENUES**.

**Napoleon (1769-1821):** Probably the most famous ruler of France there has ever been. He was the son of a Corsican nobleman who rose through the ranks of the Revolutionary Army to become a brigadier at the age of 24. In 1799 he seized power in a coup d'état, and crowned himself the first Emperor of France (1804).
His attempt to conquer the whole of Europe was finally crushed at the Battle of Waterloo in 1815, and he died six years later in exile on the island of St Helena. His remains were returned to France in 1840, and now lie in the tomb in the Dôme des Invalides (see **CHURCHES**, **A-Z**).

**Newspapers:** You can buy newspapers at pavement news-kiosks, bookshops and drugstores. The French dailies include: *Le Monde,* which is authoritative, slightly left-of-centre and has no pictures; *Le Figaro,* conservative; and *Libération,* independent and left-wing.
British papers and the *International Herald Tribune* are all widely available at kiosks in the centre of Paris. It is also possible to purchase British magazines at W. H. Smith (See **SHOPPING 2**).
*Pariscope, l'Officiel des Spectacles* and *7 Jours à Paris* are magazines which appear weekly and contain comprehensive listings (all in French) of cinema, theatre, museums, art shows, restaurants, cabarets,

sport and exhibitions. They are available every Wed. (approx. 2F-3F). *Paris Passion* is a bi-monthly English-language magazine with useful information as well as cultural features on city life. See **What's On**.

**Nightlife:** There is plenty of nightlife in Paris ranging from the world-famous cabarets, like the *Lido, Moulin Rouge* (see **A-Z**), or *Folies Bergère*, to nightclubs, discos, jazz clubs and bars. The most lively areas include St-Germain-des-Prés, Les Halles, the Latin Quarter (see **CITY DISTRICTS, WALK 3, A-Z**), Rue Mouffetard (see **A-Z**), Montparnasse (see **CITY DISTRICTS, A-Z**), Montmartre (see **CITY DISTRICTS, WALK 5, A-Z**), La Pigalle (see **A-Z**), and the Champs-Élysées (see **MUSTS, A-Z**). See **NIGHTLIFE**.

**Notre Dame Cathedral:** Built between 1163 and 1345, this well-known Gothic cathedral has been the centre of many important events through the years: 1594 - conversion to Catholicism and coronation of Henri IV; 1804 - crowning of Napoleon (see **A-Z**) as first Emperor of France; 1980 - The Magnificat with Pope John Paul II.
After the Revolution the cathedral fell into neglect, but was to witness a revival with the Romantic Movement and interest generated through Victor Hugo's novel *The Hunchback of Notre Dame*, resulting in public pressure for restoration from 1841 onwards.
The western facade is the most impressive with three carved portals depicting the Virgin Mary, the Last Judgement, and St Anne. Above is the Gallery of Kings and the superb rose window. The best view of the interior is from below the organ where you can see the light flooding in through the stained glass. Try to climb to the top of the north tower where you not only have a marvellous view, but come face-to-face with the grotesque carved gargoyles. See **CHURCHES, MUSTS, WALK 1**.

**Opening Times:** *Banks*: 0900-1200, 1400-1630 Mon.-Fri. (busy central branches stay open at lunchtime).
*Chemists*: 0900-1930 Mon.-Sat.
*Offices*: 0830-12 00, 1400-1800 Mon.-Sat.
*Restaurants*: generally open 1200-1500, 1930-2230. Many close on Mon., and some close for whole month of August.
*Shops*: 1000-1900 Tues.-Sat.

**Opéra, L':** The largest opera house in the world, built by Garnier for Napoleon III and completed in 1875. Both the exterior and interior are extremely grand and ornate, and during the day there are guided tours of the inside of the building, including the underground grotto which is supposed to have inspired the story of *The Phantom of the Opera*. Tours are from 1100-1700. It is difficult to obtain tickets for performances - you will have to book at least two weeks in advance and be prepared to pay as much as 300F-600F each. See MUSIC VENUES.

**Orientation:** The city is divided from east to west by the River Seine with the Right Bank to the north and Left Bank to the south. At the city centre are the islands of Île de la Cité and Île St Louis, and the cathedral of Notre Dame. The main axis of the city lies on the Right Bank from the Louvre through the Arc de Triomphe to La Défense. Montmartre with the Sacré-Cœur is to the north of the centre; Maine-Montparnasse Tower is to the south, and the Eiffel Tower to the west. If you use these three landmarks as a guide you should always be able to find out roughly where you are in the city.

**Orsay, Musée d':** Originally the Gare d'Orsay railway station, today this building houses an art gallery for paintings and sculptures dating from 1848-1914, including a collection of over 700 Impressionist works previously kept in the Jeu de Paume. See ART GALLERIES.

**Panthéon:** Dedicated to Ste Geneviève, and built by Louis XV, this mausoleum for heroes of the French Republic is the last resting place of Victor Hugo, Émile Zola, Rousseau, Voltaire, Louis Braille and Resistance leader Jean Moulin. Place du Panthéon, 5e. RER/M Luxembourg, Cardinal-Lemoine. See WALK 3.

**Passports and Customs:** A passport from Britain, Ireland or the EC allows a 90-day stay and no visa is required. Also acceptable are British Visitors Passports and Excursion Passes (available from Post Offices). If you wish to stay for more than 90 days, contact the local police station in France, or Préfecture de Police (*Service des Étrangers*), 7-9 bd du Palais, Paris 4e. Citizens from other countries, including the

USA, Canada, Australia and New Zealand, require a visa, which is eas-
ily obtained from French embassies and consulates in those countries.
*Australia*: French Consulate, St Martin Tower, 31 Manet St., Sydney
NSW 2000. Tel: 328 1250. Embassy in Canberra, Consulate in
Melbourne.
*Canada*: French Embassy, 42 Promenade Sussex, Ottawa, Ontario K1M
2C9. Tel: 512 1715. Consulates in Toronto, Edmonton and Montreal.
*New Zealand:* French Embassy, 1 Williston Street, DBP 1695,
Wellington. Tel: 720 200.
*UK*: French Embassy, 58 Knightsbridge, London SW1. Tel: 235 8080.
Consulates in Liverpool and Edinburgh.
*USA*: French Embassy, 4101 Reservoir Road NY, Washington DC,
20007. Tel: 94 46000. Consulates in Boston, Chicago, Miami, New
York, San Francisco.

**Pets:** If you take your pets to France from the UK, they are required by
law to spend six months in quarantine on re-entry to the UK.

**Pigalle:** This is a sleazy red-light district below Montmartre (see CITY
DISTRICTS, MUSTS, WALK 5, **A-Z**),with sex-shops, porn cinemas and pros-
titutes. Stretching west from place Pigalle is the busy bd de Clichy with
restaurants and the famous Théâtre des Deux Ânes at no. 100. The
notorious Moulin Rouge (see **A-Z**) is situated on place Blanche.
9e/18e. M Pigalle, Blanche, Place Clichy. See NIGHTLIFE.

**Police:** The police can be recognized by their dark blue uniforms and
flat caps. Always address them as '*M'sieur l'Agent*' - they are usually
considerate to tourists. Any theft should be reported to the nearest
police station (*commissariat de police*). The Police HQ in Paris is at 51
pl du Marché-St-Honoré, 1er. See **Crime and Theft, Emergencies**.

**Pompidou Centre:** Its full title is: Centre National d'Art et de
Culture Georges-Pompidou. This massive, ultra-modern building by
controversial architects Richard Rogers (UK) and Renzo Piano (Italy)
was opened in 1977 to house a 'multi-cultural centre'. It consists of five
storeys of glass and steel, with structural members, ventilation shafts

and escalators on the outside, and painted bright red, yellow, green and blue. Inside are the Musée National d'Art Moderne (see **ART GALLERIES**), a library, exhibition halls, art bookshop and two research institutes. Plateau Beaubourg, 4e. M Rambuteau. 1200-2200 Mon.,Wed., Thurs., Fri. 1000-2200. Sat., Sun. Free, except for Musée and some exhibitions.

**Pompidou, Georges (1911-74):** French statesman who succeeded de Gaulle (see **A-Z**) as president in 1969. He reversed de Gaulle's policy of resistance to British membership of the Common Market, and was instrumental in securing acceptance of Britain's entry to the Community in 1973 after years of negotiation.

**Post Offices:** Normally open 0900-1900 Mon.-Fri., 0800-1200 Sat. They can be identified by their yellow signs marked 'PTT' or 'Postes', and provide full postal facilities as well as telephones for both local and long-distance calls. These can be metered and paid for afterwards (see **Telephones and Telegrams**). Postage stamps can also be purchased from *tabacs* (see **Cigarettes and Tobacco**). Parisian letter-boxes are painted yellow.
The Head Post Office (open 24 hrs a day) is at Hôtel des Postes, 52 rue du Louvre, 1er. M Louvre, M/RER Châtelet-les-Halles.
*Poste restante*: any mail to be picked up should be clearly addressed with your name and '*Poste Restante*', then sent to the Hôtel des Postes (see above). You will have to produce your passport before collecting any mail from *Poste Restante.*

**Public Holidays:** 1 January; Easter Sun. and Mon.; Ascension (40 days after Easter); Pentecost (7th Sun. after Easter plus the following Mon.); 1 May (Labour Day); 8 May (Armistice Day 1945); 14 July (Bastille Day - see **Quatorze Juillet**); 15 August (Assumption of Virgin Mary); 1 November (All Saints Day); 11 November (Armistice Day 1918); 25 December (Christmas Day).

**Quartier Juif:** The Jewish Quarter, chiefly concentrated around the rue des Rosiers in the 4e *arr.*, with many kosher shops and restaurants. M St-Paul-le Marais. See **WALK 2**.

**Quatorze Juillet, Fête Nationale de:** Bastille Day, 14 July - France's national holiday, commemorating the storming of the Bastille (see **A-Z**). Everything closes and the whole country joins in the celebrations, including firework displays, parties and military processions along the Champs-Élysées. See **Events**.

**Railways:** The RER (*Réseau Express Régional* - Regional Express Network) is linked to the *Métro* (see **A-Z**) and has three lines (A, B and C) connecting the city to the suburbs and outlying areas. Note that for Zone 1 it uses the same ticket system as the *Métro* (supplementary tickets are required for travel to the suburbs).

The SNCF (*Société Nationale des Chemins de Fer Français*) is the national network, which provides a fast, comfortable service. Paris has six mainline stations: Gare du Nord (for Boulogne, Calais, Belgium, Holland and Scandinavia); Gare de l'Est (for eastern France, Germany, Switzerland, Austria); Gare St-Lazare (for Dieppe, Normandy); Gare de Lyon (for the Alps, South of France, Italy, Greece); Gare d'Austerlitz (for the south-west, Spain, Portugal); Gare Montparnasse (for Brittany, Versailles, Chartres, Atlantic coast).

Stations have all the usual facilities, including currency exchange, shops and Tourist Information Offices. Reservations are recommended for long-distance journeys, and you can buy either first or second class tickets. You must then punch the ticket in the machine on the platform before boarding the train. If you don't do this and are asked to produce the ticket by an inspector, you may be charged for another one.

For general railway enquiries tel: 42.61.50.50.

**Religious Services:** France is predominantly a Catholic country, and details and times of services can be obtained from the Centre d'Information et de Documentation Religieuse, 8 rue Massillon, 4e. Tel: 46.33.01.01.

*Anglican*: St George's Church, 7 rue Auguste Vacquerie, 16e.
*Church of Scotland*: 17 rue Bayard, 8e.
*Protestant*: American Church, 65 quai d'Orsay, 7e.
*Jewish*: Association Israélite de Paris, 17 rue St-Georges, 9e.
*Moslem*: Mosquée de Paris, pl du Puits-de-l'Ermite, 5e.

**Right Bank:** A commercial district lying to the north of the Seine (see **A-Z**) where most of the Parisian offices and businesses are to be found. It is situated between the Jardins des Tuileries (see **PARKS**) and l'Opéra (see **MUSIC VENUES**, **A-Z**), extending from L'Étoile (see **A-Z**) to Beaubourg (see **CITY DISTRICTS**).

**Rivoli, rue de:** A well-known shopping street, now overrun with souvenir shops. There are also tea-rooms, grand hotels and W. H. Smith (newsagent and bookshop). The arcade section, running from place de la Concorde (see **A-Z**) and the Louvre (see **ART GALLERIES, MUSEUMS 1, MUSTS, A-Z**), was built to celebrate Napoleon's (see **A-Z**) victories in Italy. 1er. M Concorde, Tuileries-Palais Royal. See **SHOPPING 2 & 3**.

**Sacré-Cœur:** This magnificent white basilica was built by public subscription in 1876-91 as an act of contrition and expression of hope following France's disasters in the Franco-Prussian War of 1870-71. It was consecrated in 1919 and stands in a prominent position on top of the Butte de Montmartre, making it a familiar landmark. See **CHURCHES, WALK 5, Montmartre**.

**Saint-Denis Basilica:** Situated in the northern suburb of St-Denis, this 12thC cathedral marked the birth of Gothic architecture in Europe, and the first-ever rose window in its western front was to become a standard feature of Gothic churches. The cathedral has been the traditional setting for the crowning of French Kings, and the tombs of all but three are contained here. M St-Denis-Basilique. See **EXCURSIONS 1**.

**Sainte Chapelle:** Originally built in 1243-48 as a shrine for holy relics and restored in the 19thC. It is best known for its stained glass scenes from the Old and New Testament, and the 15thC rose window which portrays scenes from the Apocalypse. See **CHURCHES, WALK 1**.

**Saint-Germain-des-Prés:** Dating from the 6thC, this is the oldest church in Paris and was initially a Benedictine abbey before being rebuilt during the 11th, 12th and 17thC. It was extensively restored in 1822 after an explosion and fire, and today hosts a mixture of Romanesque, Gothic and 19thC decoration. Pl St-Germain-des-Prés, 6e. M St-Germain-des-Prés. See **CHURCHES, WALK 3, Left Bank**.

**Saint-Germain-en-Laye:** The château is now the home of the excellent Musée des Antiquités Nationales with its impressive collection of objects and artefacts from Stone Age to Roman and Merovingian

St -Germain- en -Laye

times. In the Stone Age section is a model of the famous Lascaux Caves where the earliest examples of cave-paintings were found. 0745-1200.1330-1715 Wed.-Mon. 15F. 21 km west of the city. RER St-Germain-en-Laye. See **EXCURSIONS 2**.

**Saint Sulpice:** 17th-18thC church with imposing western front and splendid organ, one of the largest in the world. Look out for the meridian line engraved between the transcepts. It is lit by the sun's rays at noon on different points depending on the time of year. See **CHURCHES**.

**Seine:** The river which starts near Dijon to the south of Paris and flows for 771 km to the sea at Le Havre. An 11 km stretch flows through Paris with its famous waterfront - *quais de Paris*. Today the right bank has been taken over by a cross-city motorway, but the left bank has been left relatively unspoilt and you can still enjoy romantic strolls on its cobbled quays.

**Shopping:** Paris has something for everyone, from the bookstalls (*bouquinistes*) along the Seine to the exclusive fashion houses. The

main shopping areas are Les Halles (all kinds), Boulevard Haussmann (department stores), rue Faubourg-St-Honoré (high fashion), rue Royale (expensive jewellery), rue de Rivoli (perfume, souvenirs), and, on the Left Bank (see **CITY DISTRICTS, MUSTS, WALK 3**, A-Z), the St-Germain-des-Prés area (books, antiques, art, fashion). See **MARKETS, SHOPPING**.

**Sorbonne, La:** Founded in 1253 by Robert de Sorbon, this one-time theological college is now one of the world's greatest universities. Student unrest here in 1968 led to university reform in France. 17 rue de la Sorbonne, 5e. M Odéon, RER Luxembourg. See **WALK 3**.

**Sports:** Details of current sports events and facilities are well covered in *Pariscope* or *Paris Passion* (see **Newspapers, What's On**), or the telephone information service Allô Sports, tel: 42.76.54.54. Football and rugby (internationals in Feb. and Mar.) at Parc des Princes, 24 rue du Commandant Guilbaud, 16e; International Tennis Championships in June at Stade Roland-Garros, av Gordon-Benett, 16e;

the finish of the Tour de France cycle race in mid-July along the Champs-Élysées; horse-racing at Longchamp (Prix de l'Arc de Triomphe and Prix de la République in Oct.) and Auteuil (see **Bois de Boulogne**), trotting races at Vincennes (Aug.-Sept.).

**Taxis:** Paris boasts 14,300 official taxis which can be either picked up at one of the numerous taxi ranks, or ordered by phone. Within the *boulevard périphérique* (ring road), there are two tariffs: 'A' - 2,55F/km, 0700-2000; 'B' - 3,97F/km, 2000-0700 and all day Sun. and hols. For trips outside the ring-road, tariff 'B' applies 0700-2000, and tariff 'C' (5,33F/km) 2000-0700. Supplementary charges of 3F or 4F apply for taxis at mainline railway stations, for luggage, and for more than three passengers. Tipping (see **A-Z**) is normal but not obligatory.
*G7 Radio* - tel: 47.39.47.39;
*Taxis-Bleus* - tel: 42.02.42.02;
*Alpha-Taxis* - tel: 47.30.23.23;
*Taxis Radio-Étoile* - tel: 42.70.41.41.

**Telephones and Telegrams:** You will find numerous pay-phones but you may have difficulty finding one to accept money rather than phonecards. Coin-operated phones take 1F, 5F and occasionally 10F coins. Phonecards (*Télécartes*) are available from post offices and *tabacs* and cost 45F and 96F. To use a card phone, lift the receiver, insert card, pull down the handle above it and dial. For coin-operated phones, insert the money first, then dial. In post offices (see **A-Z**) you can use a metered phone which lets you make the call before paying. If using a café phone, you may have to buy a *jeton* (token) at the bar. When dialing inside Paris you need only use the eight digits. For calls to the rest of the country dial 16, and then the area code and number. For international calls dial 19, wait for dialling tone, then country code (44 for UK, 61 for Australia, 11 for USA), followed by the area code (omitting the initial zero) and number.

If you wish to make a reverse-charge call abroad, dial 19.33 then the country code to get through to a bilingual operator. You can receive return calls at phone booths.

Telegrams: this service is available at post offices. Also by telephone: inside France, dial 36.15, and dictate (in French). For abroad, dial 42.33.21.11. (in English).

**Television and Radio:** There are 6 channels on French TV: TF1, A2, FR3, La5, M6 and Canal+ (the first paying and coded network). By 1992 cable TV will cater for as many as 30 channels. The news is broadcast at 0800, 1300, 2000 and 2300.

French radio broadcasts in French on FM. The best-known stations are: France-Inter, France Musique, France Culture, Radio Tour Eiffel, Skyrock, NRJ, Radio Classique, RTL, Europe1.

It is possible to receive BBC Radio 4 by tuning in to 1500 m long wave, and BBC World Service on 463 m medium wave.

All Parisian FM radio stations are listed in *Pariscope* (see **Newspapers, What's On**).

**Time Differences:** French standard time is GMT plus one hour, and the clocks go forward an hour in summer, making France (like the rest of Western Europe) always one hour ahead of Britain.

**Tipping:** A 15% service charge is included in your bill at all hotels and restaurants, so there is no need to leave anything unless you feel the service has been particularly good, in which case a small tip of 10F for the waiter is appropriate. If you pay by cash, any small change is usually left for the waiter, hotel porters average 10F for each item of luggage, chambermaids 10F per day, taxi drivers 10-15% of the fare, hairdressers about 10F, and cinema usherettes normally 1F.

**Tourist Information:** The main Tourist Information Office is at 127 av des Champs-Élysées, 8e, near the Arc de Triomphe (0900-2200 Mon.-Sat., 0900-1800 Sun). You'll find the staff speak English and are both helpful and friendly. They are well stocked with free maps and leaflets giving information on accommodation, restaurants, exhibitions, entertainments, transport and excursions. You can also buy guide books and maps in the bookshop. Other Tourist Information Offices can be found at the following railway stations: Gare d'Austerlitz, Gare de l'Est, Gare de Lyon and Gare du Nord. Tourist information in English is available by telephone 47.20.88.98.The French Government Tourist Office in the UK is at 178 Piccadilly, London W1V OAL, tel: 01-493 6594.

**Transport:** Paris has one of the best public transport systems in the world. The RATP (*Régie Autonome des Transports Parisiens*) run the interlinked *Métro*, bus and RER, which serve the city and the suburbs. The system is fast, easy to use, and very well signposted - in fact it is almost impossible to get lost on the *Métro*. Inter-city and international rail services are provided by the SNCF, from six mainline stations. The two airports which serve Paris are connected to the city by a fast and frequent bus and rail service. See **Airports**, **Buses**, **Métro**, **Railways**.

**Vendôme, Place:** A magnificent 17th-18thC square which retains the original facades designed by Hardouin-Mansart. The buildings now house luxury shops and hotels, including the Ritz. At the centre of the square is the Vendôme Column, which was built in 1806-10 in the style of Trajan's Column in Rome. It has bronze bas-reliefs celebrating the military exploits of Napoleon (see **A-Z**), with a statue of the Emperor himself on top. See **WALK 4**.

**Versailles:** It was originally a hunting lodge favoured by Louis XIII and transformed into the sumptuous palace as we know it by Louis XIV. No expense was spared and building continued for over half-a-century supervised by the masters Le Vau as architect, Le Brun as decorator and Le Nôtre as garden designer. The latter's task was no easy one as it involved draining the marshy land, diverting the River Bièvre to supply the 1,400 fountains and planting 150,000 plants. After the Revolution the castle fell into disrepair, the furniture was sold and the paintings removed. It was saved by King Louis-Philippe, who created the Museum of the History of France there in 1873, and restoration work has continued ever since, particularly from the 1950s.
See **EXCURSION 3.**

**What's On:** The most useful listings publications with information on what's on are: *Pariscope* (weekly, 3F, in French), and *l'Officiel des Spectacles* (weekly, 2F). You'll also find the magazine *Paris Passion* helpful (bi-monthly, in English). It includes features on city life and an information section. All are easily obtained from kiosks and newsagents. See **Newspapers**.

**Youth Hostels:** The YHA in France is the *Auberges de Jeunesse Français*, 12 rue des Barres, 4e. Tel: 42.72.72.09. There are two hostels in the city itself, though you will have to hold an international YHA membership to use them. In summer it is best to book in advance by sending a letter with a cheque or postal order for 50F.

*Jules Ferry*, 8 bd Jules-Ferry 11e. Tel: 43.57.55.60. M République.
*D'Artagnon*, 80 rue Vitruve 20e. Tel: 43.61.08.75. M Porte de Bagnolet. The cost is 53F/night, which includes breakfast. The youth organisation *Accueil des Jeunes en France* (AJF) also runs a chain of fine city hostels costing 62F/night. Although no membership is necessary for these, they are restricted to 18-30 year olds, and don't accept bookings ahead so be prepared to take a chance.

AJF hostels:
*Résidence Bastille,* 151 av Ledru-Rollin 11e. Tel: 43.79.53.86.M Bastille,Voltaire. *Le Fourcy,* 6 rue de Fourcy 4e. Tel: 42.74.23.45.M St-Paul. *Le Fauconnier,* 11 rue du Fauconnie 4e. Tel: 42.74.23.45.M Pont Marie. *Maubuisson,* 12 rue des Barres 4e. Tel: 42.72.72.09.M Hôtel de Ville. *François Miron,* 6 rue François-Miron 4e. Tel: 42.72.72.09.M Hôtel de Ville.

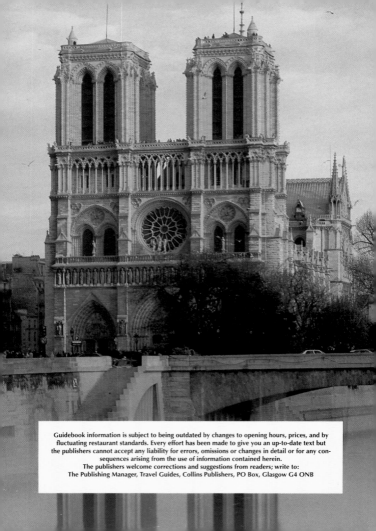